NAVIGATING
Docker

**From Setup to Deployment:
A Developer's Companion**

Ethan Calderwood

TABLE OF CONTENTS

INTRODUCTION

The tools we use in software development are constantly changing to allow for more productivity, enhanced functionality, and more seamless workflows. Among these tools, Docker is particularly noteworthy for being a game-changer, altering how we develop, construct, and use applications.

Welcome to " Navigating Docker: From Setup to Deployment - A Developer's Companion". This e-book will serve as your map to help you navigate the vast sea of containerization. This e-book is designed with you in mind, regardless of your level of experience—from a total novice who has never heard the term "Docker" to an intermediate developer looking to strengthen your knowledge and abilities.

We shall go on a journey through the pages of this e-book that begins at the very core of Docker, explaining its design and the main ways it differs from conventional virtual machines. We'll delve into every detail of this potent platform, from configuring Docker on your local computer to learning about Dockerfiles, container management, networking, and more.

But we won't confine our exploration to the fundamentals. We'll get into more complex subjects, including integrating Docker into your continuous integration and deployment pipelines, guaranteeing the security of your containers, and optimizing Docker images. Furthermore, real-world case studies will enhance your learning process by providing insights into effective Docker installations.

It's now essential to understand Docker in the ever-changing software industry. Upon finishing the e-book, you will have acquired the necessary knowledge and abilities to fully utilize Docker, guaranteeing that your applications are not only dependable and efficient but also scalable, portable, and resilient.

Come along on this insightful voyage into the Docker world with us, and you'll leave a more knowledgeable, capable, and self-assured developer. Let's dive in!

CHAPTER I

Docker Basics

Docker architecture

In the vast landscape of modern software development, Docker has emerged as a beacon, signaling a shift towards more efficient, reliable, and reproducible builds. Central to Docker's widespread adoption and success is its innovative architecture. Understanding this architecture is not just a theoretical exercise; it's a practical necessity for those wishing to harness Docker's full potential.

At the heart of Docker's architecture is the concept of containerization. Unlike traditional virtualization, which replicates the entire operating system to run an application, containerization encapsulates an application and its dependencies into a 'container.' This approach offers several advantages: it's lightweight, fast, and ensures the application runs consistently across different environments. But what makes containerization so efficient? The answer lies in Docker's architecture.

Docker employs a client-server architecture. The Docker daemon, which performs the labor-intensive task of creating, launching, and maintaining Docker containers, is in communication with the Docker client. The Docker client can interact with a daemon running on a different host, or both the client and the daemon can operate on the same system. Communication between the Docker client and the Docker daemon happens over a REST API, UNIX sockets, or a network interface.

A crucial component of Docker's architecture is the Docker Image. Think of an image as a lightweight, stand-alone, executable software package that includes everything required to run a piece of software, including the code, runtime, system tools, libraries, and settings. Images are portable across any system that runs Docker. Containers, however, are active runtime instances of these images. When a user wants to run a container based on an image, the Docker daemon takes the image, adds a writable file system on top, and initializes various settings (including network ports, container name, ID and resource limits) before running the container as an isolated process in user space on the host operating system.

A pivotal advantage of Docker's architecture comes from its layered approach to images. When an image is built, each operation is represented as a layer. These layers are stacked on top of each other to form the final image. Only the modified layer is rebuilt when changes are made, and the unchanged layers are reused. This makes builds faster and ensures that images, especially those sharing common layers, are storage-efficient. Combined with the lightweight nature of containers, this layered approach makes it possible to run multiple containers simultaneously on a host, each sharing the same OS kernel but operating in isolated user spaces.

The underlying technology powering Docker's containerization is primarily rooted in Linux. Features such as namespaces and cgroups, native to the Linux kernel, play a pivotal role. Namespaces ensure the isolation of containers, meaning each container has its own isolated file system, networking, and process list. This makes containers unaware of each other's existence, ensuring security and autonomy. On the other hand, cgroups, or control groups, regulate and monitor the resource allocation to containers, ensuring that no single container can monopolize system resources.

Networking is another sophisticated facet of Docker's architecture. Docker, by default, provides a bridge network for containers, ensuring they can communicate with each other and with the external world. However, Docker's networking capabilities don't stop there. It also offers host networking and overlay networks and allows users to define their custom networks. This flexibility in networking options caters to a wide range of use cases, from standalone containers to multi-container applications spanning multiple hosts in clustered environments.

A discussion of Docker's architecture would be incomplete without mentioning Docker Compose and Docker Swarm. While not core to the primary architecture, they enhance and extend Docker's capabilities. Docker Compose lets developers to define and run multi-container Docker applications using a simple YAML file, streamlining the container orchestration process. On the other hand, Docker Swarm is Docker's native clustering and scheduling tool. It translates a pool of Docker hosts into a single virtual host, providing load balancing and ensuring high availability.

In conclusion, Docker's architecture represents a paradigm shift in how applications are developed, shipped, and run. It decouples applications from the infrastructure, ensuring consistency, scalability, and resilience. Its client-server model, combined with the efficiency of images and containers, offers a seamless experience to developers and operators alike. The underlying Linux features ensure isolation and resource management, while flexible networking options cater to many application needs. As Docker continues to evolve and reshape the software world, a solid grasp of its architecture will remain indispensable for any modern developer or system administrator.

The difference between containers and virtual machines

In the evolving landscape of software deployment and infrastructure management, two terms often arise as prominent game-changers: containers and virtual machines (VMs). Both are groundbreaking in their rights and have carved significant niches within the IT domain. But despite their shared goals of isolating applications and making software more reproducible across different environments, they differ fundamentally in design and application. This section delves deep into the distinctions between these two paradigms.

Virtual machines have been the go-to solution for infrastructure management for many years. Conceptually, a VM is like an independent computer running on another computer. At the VM ecosystem's foundation is a host system's physical hardware. Above this, a hypervisor (or virtual machine monitor) sits, acting as a layer responsible for creating, running, and managing multiple VMs. Each

VM encapsulates an entire environment with its operating system, libraries, binaries, and applications. This encapsulation ensures complete isolation; a VM runs unaffected by other VMs on the same host and can seamlessly move across host systems.

Containers, conversely, introduce a more streamlined approach to isolation. They encapsulate the application and its dependencies but share the host system's operating system kernel. This means containers are inherently lighter than VMs, as they don't carry the overhead of an entire OS. Docker, one of the leading containerization platforms, popularized this approach, allowing developers to "package" applications with all their dependencies into standardized units.

One of the most pronounced differences between VMs and containers is their size and speed. Given that a VM hosts a full-fledged OS, it demands significant system resources. Its boot-up sequence includes starting an entire operating system, which naturally takes time. Containers, by contrast, are lightweight, housing only the application and its direct dependencies. They begin almost instantaneously, making them especially suited for environments where rapid scaling or high density is a priority.

Another pivotal distinction is the approach to isolation. While both VMs and containers offer isolated environments, achieving this isolation varies. VMs rely on the hypervisor to provide hard isolation. Each VM operates as if it's the only entity on the hardware, unaware of the existence of its peers. Containers, leveraging features of the host OS, employ a softer form of isolation. Technologies like

Linux namespaces ensure each container operates in its isolated user space. This means that while containers are isolated, they are more intertwined with the host system than VMs.

Management and orchestration also differ between these two realms. Traditional VM management tools, such as VMware's vSphere or Microsoft's Hyper-V, focus on VM provisioning, lifecycle management, and resource allocation tasks. As VMs are hefty entities, these tools prioritize stability and long-term management. However, container orchestration platforms, like Kubernetes, deal with ephemeral, lightweight entities. They emphasize rapid deployment, scaling, and resilience. The paradigm here shifts from long-lived, stable entities to short-lived, flexible ones that can be spun up or down based on demand.

Efficiency and resource utilization are areas where containers typically outshine VMs. Because containers share the host OS kernel and avoid the overhead of running multiple OS instances, they consume fewer system resources. This efficiency means one can run many more containers than VMs on a host system, maximizing hardware utilization. Conversely, VMs offer a broader compatibility range since they encapsulate entire operating systems. A VM can run an OS entirely different from the host's OS, while a container is, to an extent, bound by the host's OS environment.

Lastly, the security models of VMs and containers diverge significantly. VMs, given their hard isolation, offer a robust security boundary. Even if an attacker compromise one VM, breaking out of its confines to affect the host or other VMs is exceptionally challenging. Containers, being more intertwined with the host OS, have a thinner security boundary. While modern containers offer substantial security features, their nature makes them slightly more susceptible to breakout scenarios.

In conclusion, while containers and virtual machines revolutionize software deployment and management, they cater to different needs and scenarios. VMs, with their robust isolation and comprehensive environments, are suited for long-term, stable deployments. Containers, with their lightweight, efficient design, cater to dynamic, scalable environments where agility is paramount. As with many technological choices, the decision between VMs and containers isn't a matter of absolute superiority but of appropriateness to the task at hand.

CHAPTER II

Setting Up Docker

Prerequisites

Docker's emergence as a leading platform for containerization has transformed how developers package, distribute, and deploy applications. Its promise of ensuring consistency across various environments - "Build Once, Run Anywhere" - has undoubtedly been a significant draw. However, one must be prepared before delving into the world of Docker containers. Understanding and setting up the prerequisites are crucial to ensuring a smooth, efficient, and effective Docker experience.

At its core, Docker is essentially a tool that allows applications to run inside containers. These containers are isolated, lightweight environments that share the host system's operating system kernel but have their application, libraries, and dependencies. Given this intricate dance between host and container, compatibility is the primary concern before setting up Docker.

The host operating system plays a pivotal role in Docker's operations. Initially, Docker was native to Linux, leveraging Linux-specific features like cgroups and namespaces for its core functionalities.

Thus, a primary prerequisite was a Linux-based OS, be it Ubuntu, CentOS, or Fedora. Over time, however, Docker expanded its horizons. For Windows and Mac users, Docker Desktop has been introduced. This software provides a seamless Docker experience on non-Linux platforms by employing a virtual machine in the background. Therefore, one of the first steps in preparing for Docker is ensuring that your OS is supported and you have the appropriate version.

Yet, the software's demands do not end at the operating system. There are hardware considerations to account for. Docker requires a 64-bit processor with virtualization capabilities. Most modern CPUs come equipped with this, but verifying that virtualization is enabled in the BIOS or UEFI settings is essential. Additionally, while Docker can run on systems with minimal RAM, having at least 4GB is recommended. This ensures that you can run multiple containers simultaneously without facing performance bottlenecks.

Network connectivity is another essential aspect. Docker images, which are the templates from which containers are instantiated, are often stored on Docker Hub or other container registries. To pull these images, a stable internet connection is necessary. Moreover, when communicating with external services or other containers, Docker containers rely on networking. Thus, understanding and configuring host firewalls or proxies becomes a key preparatory step.

Beyond these foundational requirements, there are optional yet often beneficial prerequisites. A notable mention here is the storage configuration. Docker stores its images and containers on the host's primary storage by default. But considering external storage solutions or configuring Docker to utilize a different storage driver can be worthwhile in scenarios where large images are involved or storage is at a premium. Similarly, while Docker comes with a default bridge network, understanding and possibly setting up custom networks, especially in complex applications, is a valuable endeavor.

A sound understanding of command-line interfaces (CLI) cannot be overstressed. While Docker does offer graphical user interfaces (like Docker Desktop), much of Docker's power and flexibility lie in its CLI. Commands for building images, starting or stopping containers, inspecting logs, and managing networks are primarily executed through the terminal. Therefore, familiarizing oneself with basic CLI operations and syntax, pertinent to their operating system, is invaluable.

Docker's ecosystem doesn't exist in isolation. Often, it intertwines with other software tools and platforms. For developers or teams looking to integrate Docker into their development pipelines, prerequisites extend to understanding integration points with continuous integration and continuous deployment (CI/CD) tools like Jenkins, GitLab CI, or Travis CI. Similarly, if Docker is to be part of a more extensive orchestration system, familiarity with platforms like Kubernetes becomes relevant.

Lastly, while not a technical requirement, cultivating a mindset of containerization is perhaps one of the most significant prerequisites. Traditionally, developers thought about applications running directly on physical or virtualized hardware. Docker introduces an intermediate layer - the container. Designing applications for this environment, understanding the principles of microservices, and recognizing the patterns and antipatterns of containerized deployments can significantly impact the success of Docker implementations.

In conclusion, Docker's allure lies in its promise of consistency, scalability, and portability. Yet, as with any powerful tool, its effective use demands preparation. Whether it's ensuring hardware and software compatibility, gearing up for network and storage considerations, or embracing the nuances of container-centric design, these prerequisites set the stage for a rewarding Docker journey. As technology continues its relentless march forward, tools like Docker redefine software development and deployment paradigms. Being prepared ensures that we navigate these changes and truly harness their potential.

Installation on various platforms (Windows, Mac, Linux)

With its revolutionary approach to software deployment using containerization, Docker has garnered widespread acceptance among developers and IT professionals. Yet, an essential facet of Docker's broad appeal is its ability to run across various platforms, each having its nuances and procedures. Delving into the installation of Docker on Windows, Mac, and Linux elucidates the unique steps and considerations, offering a holistic perspective on bringing Docker's power to diverse computing environments.

Docker's journey on the Windows platform has evolved dramatically. Initially, leveraging Docker on Windows required virtual machines running Linux, since Docker's core relied heavily on Linux-specific features. This changed with the introduction of Docker Desktop for Windows. Powered by Microsoft's Hyper-V technology, Docker Desktop provides a near-native Docker experience on Windows without the complexities of managing a separate Linux VM.

To install Docker on Windows, users must first ensure they operate on Windows 10 Pro, Enterprise, or Education editions. Docker Desktop relies on Hyper-V, which is unavailable in Windows Home editions. Users can download the Docker Desktop installer from the Docker website after verifying system compatibility and ensuring virtualization is enabled in the BIOS settings. Docker runs as a service post-installation, providing a seamless integration with the Windows environment. It's worth noting that Microsoft and Docker have collaborated to introduce Windows Containers, allowing for the containerization of Windows-native applications, though Linux-based containers remain more prevalent.

Like its Windows counterpart, Docker Desktop for Mac offers a streamlined experience for macOS users. Underneath, Docker Desktop for Mac harnesses the power of a lightweight virtual machine to run Docker, but this complexity remains hidden, providing users with a transparent, native-feel experience.

Before embarking on the installation journey on Mac, ensuring that one is running macOS Sierra 10.12 or a newer version is pivotal.

Given these criteria, installing Docker becomes a straightforward affair. Users can download the Docker.dmg file from the Docker website, which, once executed, installs Docker and its dependencies. Like the Windows platform, Docker operates in the background as a service post-installation, integrating smoothly with the macOS ecosystem. One notable feature of Docker on Mac is its ability to handle file system events efficiently, which is crucial for developers using live-reload features in their applications.

Linux, being Docker's birthplace, offers a more native, integrated experience. Given Docker's initial design around Linux features like cgroups and namespaces, it's no surprise that Docker on Linux doesn't rely on virtual machines. Instead, it operates directly on the Linux kernel. This direct operation translates to performance benefits and a deeper level of integration with the host OS.

The installation process on Linux, however, varies based on the distribution. For popular distributions like Ubuntu, Docker offers a repository that users can add to their system. After updating local package databases, Docker can be installed using the package manager, typically "apt" for Debian-based distributions like Ubuntu. For other distributions, like CentOS or Fedora, the process involves adding Docker's repository suitable for the respective package manager and then installing. It's crucial to note that Docker runs as a daemon post-installation, and users might need to start this service explicitly. Additionally, it's common practice, for security reasons, to manage Docker as a non-root user, which involves adding the user to the "docker" group.

Across all platforms, once Docker is installed, verification is a recommended step. Running a simple command like docker run hello-world ensures that Docker is set up correctly and can pull images from Docker Hub and execute containers. Additionally, the platforms offer tooling and interfaces specific to their environment. For example, Docker Desktop for Windows and Mac provides a GUI allowing users to manage images, containers, and settings conveniently.

In conclusion, Docker's cross-platform capabilities underscore its versatility and broad appeal. Whether operating on the familiar terrains of Linux or navigating the realms of Windows or Mac, Docker has paved the way. While each platform has its peculiarities and steps, the overarching principle remains: Docker strives to offer a consistent, efficient containerization experience. By understanding the installation nuances of each environment, one can harness Docker's full potential, ensuring that applications remain consistent, scalable, and isolated, regardless of where they're executed.

Docker Hub and its importance

In today's technology ecosystem, the concept of containerization, championed by Docker, has revolutionized how software applications are developed, deployed, and scaled. This transformative approach to software delivery demanded a centralized platform to facilitate the dissemination of containerized applications—a role Docker Hub impeccably fulfills. As we dive deeper into Docker Hub's universe, its critical importance in the containerized software lifecycle becomes palpable, underscoring its position as a pivotal player in the Docker ecosystem.

At its core, Docker Hub is a cloud-based registry service—a repository for Docker images. These images serve as blueprints for Docker containers, encapsulating an application and its associated dependencies. By hosting these images, Docker Hub has become the de facto marketplace for developers and organizations to share and distribute their containerized applications. Whether you're a solo developer seeking a base image to kickstart your application or an enterprise sourcing a specialized software tool, Docker Hub is often the first port of call.

A distinct advantage of Docker Hub lies in its democratized approach to software sharing. Open-source contributors and global tech giants have a platform to share their creations with the world. This egalitarian ethos fosters collaboration, allowing developers to build upon others' work, leading to rapid software iteration and innovation. For instance, a developer can easily pull an official Node.js image, add their application code, and then push the resultant image back to Docker Hub publicly or privately for deployment or further collaboration. This streamlined process, where the cumbersome aspects of software setup are abstracted away, accelerates the software development lifecycle.

However, Docker Hub isn't just a passive storage solution. It's imbued with features that cater to modern software development needs. Automated builds are a prime example. With this feature, developers can link their GitHub or Bitbucket repositories to Docker

Hub. Subsequent code changes in these repositories automatically trigger a new image build in Docker Hub, ensuring that the latest version of an application is always available for deployment. This tight integration with version control platforms exemplifies Docker Hub's commitment to facilitating a seamless Continuous Integration and Continuous Deployment (CI/CD) pipeline.

Security is paramount in the age of cyber threats, and Docker Hub does not treat it as an afterthought. Image scanning, a relatively recent addition, inspects images for known vulnerabilities, notifying developers and providing them with insights to address potential threats. By proactively highlighting vulnerabilities, Docker Hub reinforces its position as an image repository and a comprehensive platform ensuring the safe and secure deployment of containerized applications.

For enterprises with bespoke requirements, Docker Hub offers tailored solutions. Private repositories, for instance, allow organizations to store their proprietary images securely, ensuring that only authorized individuals have access. Additionally, organizations can avail of more extensive storage and bandwidth options, premium support, and other features that cater to their specific operational demands. These enterprise-oriented offerings underscore Docker Hub's versatility, catering to individual developers and global corporations with equal aplomb.

Yet, the importance of Docker Hub isn't solely tethered to its feature set or its repository capabilities. Its significance is intrinsically linked to the very ethos of Docker: ensuring consistency across environments. By providing a centralized repository of images, Docker Hub ensures that developers, irrespective of their location or environment, have access to the same software blueprint. This universal access mitigates the infamous "it works on my machine" problem, ensuring that what is developed in one environment runs consistently in another.

Reflecting on Docker Hub's trajectory, it's evident that its importance transcends its role as an image repository. By fostering collaboration, facilitating CI/CD, championing security, and ensuring software consistency, Docker Hub is foundational to the containerized software movement. In a world where software is constantly evolving, Docker Hub stands as a testament to the power of community-driven development and the potential of a unified platform that caters to the diverse needs of the global developer community.

In conclusion, as Docker continues its dominance in the realm of containerization, Docker Hub's importance becomes increasingly pronounced. It serves as a beacon for developers navigating the vast seas of software deployment, a platform that hosts, nurtures, safeguards, and propels containerized applications into the future. As the heart of containerized deployment, Docker Hub pulsates with the collective rhythm of developers worldwide, driving forward an era defined by collaboration, innovation, and consistency.

CHAPTER III

Docker CLI Essentials

Basic commands (run, build, push, pull)

The world of Docker, with its innovative approach to containerization, has streamlined and transformed the software deployment landscape. At the heart of this ecosystem lies a suite of commands, enabling developers to harness Docker's capabilities effectively. Focusing on the foundational quartet—run, build, push, and pull—provides an insight into Docker's modus operandi, illuminating the path for developers navigating the containerized realm.

Let's embark by exploring the run command. This command represents the essence of Docker's promise: to execute applications consistently across different environments. When a developer issues a docker run command, they are instructing Docker to instantiate a container from a specified image. In doing so, the application encapsulated within the image springs to life, operating in an isolated environment furnished by the container. However, the command's simplicity belies its versatility. Through various flags and parameters, the run command can allocate specific system resources, mount volumes, or even link multiple containers. For instance, running a web application on a specific port or initiating a database with predefined configurations becomes feasible with the nuanced use of this command. Thus, the run command serves as the gateway to Docker's containerized world, providing developers with the tools to execute applications in a controlled, consistent, and isolated milieu.

Transitioning from execution to creation, the build command emerges as the next cornerstone. Every Docker container originates from an image, a snapshot containing the application and its dependencies. The docker build command facilitates the creation of these images. At its core, the command references a Dockerfile—a script containing a series of instructions delineating how the image should be constructed. By processing each instruction sequentially, Docker crafts an image tailored to the developer's specifications. This image then becomes the foundation for subsequent containers. A classic use-case might involve a developer defining a base operating system, installing necessary software packages, and copying the application code into the image through the Dockerfile. With the docker build command, this blueprint materializes into a tangible image, ready for deployment. The beauty of this process lies in its reproducibility. Irrespective of where the build command is executed, the resultant image remains consistent, ensuring uniformity across various stages of the software lifecycle.

With an image in tow, a developer often faces the need to share it—either with colleagues, deployment pipelines, or the broader community. This is where the push command enters the fray. Docker Hub, as discussed earlier, stands as a cloud-based repository for

Docker images. The docker push command allows developers to upload their locally crafted images to Docker Hub or any other specified registry. Once pushed, the image is globally accessible, enabling others to pull and use it. This not only fosters collaboration but also underpins Continuous Integration and Continuous Deployment pipelines. By pushing updated images to a repository, automated systems can pull these images and deploy them, ensuring that the latest version of an application is always in circulation.

Conversely, the pull command complements push, facilitating the download of Docker images from a repository to a local environment. For developers initiating their Docker journey, or those looking to utilize pre-built solutions, the docker pull command is indispensable. By simply specifying the name of the desired image, developers can download and subsequently run containers based on it. Whether it's pulling a base operating system, a specialized software tool, or an entire application stack, the pull command connects developers to a vast reservoir of containerized solutions. Moreover, in CI/CD contexts, automated systems often employ the pull command to fetch the latest application versions, ensuring synchronized deployments across various platforms.

Together, these four commands—run, build, push, and pull—form the bedrock of Docker operations. They encapsulate the lifecycle of a containerized application, from its genesis in the form of an image to its execution within a container, and its distribution across global repositories. By mastering these commands, developers unlock Docker's potential, weaving through the stages of development, testing, and deployment with grace and precision.

In conclusion, Docker's command suite offers a glimpse into its philosophy—a commitment to simplicity, consistency, and collaboration. As the tech world continues its tryst with containerization, understanding these core commands equips developers with the lexicon to converse fluently in Docker's dialect. Through these commands, Docker's promise materializes, bridging the chasm between development and deployment, individual and community, vision and reality.

Managing containers

Docker's rise to prominence in the software world owes much to its encapsulation of applications within containers. These containers provide isolated, consistent environments, ensuring applications run seamlessly across disparate platforms. But as with any revolutionary technology, the power of Docker isn't just in the creation of containers—it's in their management. Mastering container management is similar to conducting an orchestra; each container, like a musician, must play its part at the right time, in harmony with others, to produce a symphony of seamless operations.

At the core of container management lies the ability to monitor and interact with running containers. This interaction begins the moment a container is initiated with the docker run command. Once live, developers often find the need to inspect the internal workings of a container. Docker provides tools for this introspection. The docker logs command, for instance, fetches logs from a running container, offering insights into its operations. This can be invaluable when diagnosing issues or simply understanding an application's behavior.

In tandem with logs, the docker stats command provides real-time statistics about a container's resource usage, including CPU, memory, and network metrics. Together, these tools give developers a window into the heart of their containers, ensuring they remain attuned to their performance and health.

Yet, like any seasoned conductor knows, the orchestra's music isn't static; it evolves, responding to the audience and the environment. Similarly, containers might need adjustments during their lifecycle. Developers may need to enter a running container, either to explore its file system or to execute specific commands. The docker exec command is their gateway. By allowing users to run commands in active containers, it facilitates dynamic interactions, empowering developers to tweak, debug, or adapt containers in response to changing requirements.

However, only some interactions are about diving deeper into containers. Sometimes, it's about controlling their state. Starting, stopping, pausing, and restarting containers become routine tasks in a developer's workflow. Commands like docker start, docker stop, docker pause, and docker restart equip developers with granular control over container states. This control is especially crucial in production environments, where containers need to be gracefully shut down to preserve data integrity or temporarily paused to allocate resources to more pressing tasks.

As applications grow and evolve, so does the constellation of containers supporting them. It's common for modern applications to span multiple containers, each encapsulating a specific microservice or module. In such scenarios, managing individual containers can become cumbersome. Docker Compose emerges as a savior here. By allowing developers to define multi-container applications within a single file, Docker Compose streamlines the process of starting, stopping, and scaling sets of interrelated containers. This abstraction is a boon for complex projects, ensuring that the intricate dance of interdependent containers is choreographed with precision.

Yet, the lifecycle of a container isn't infinite. Over time, as applications are updated, debugged, or scaled, containers become redundant or obsolete. Here, Docker's container management tools shine again. The docker rm command allows developers to remove specific containers, ensuring that the environment remains decluttered. Additionally, with the ephemeral nature of containers—where they can be swiftly created and destroyed without residual effects—clean-up becomes an integral aspect of management. Commands like docker system prune help in this regard, removing dangling images, unused networks, and stopped containers, optimizing system resources.

Container management isn't solely about the individual. In the world of Docker, containers often find themselves as part of broader networks, connecting with other containers, databases, or external APIs. Docker's networking capabilities ensure these connections are seamless and secure. Whether it's linking two containers on the same network, exposing specific ports to the external world, or even creating isolated networks for specific application modules, Docker offers tools and commands to architect and manage these networks effectively.

In conclusion, managing Docker containers is both an art and a science. It demands a blend of technical proficiency and strategic foresight. As containers become the linchpins of modern software deployment, understanding their nuances, lifecycle, and interdependencies is paramount. Docker, with its suite of management tools, equips developers with the baton to conduct their container orchestras, ensuring that each container, from the diminutive to the dominant, plays its part in the grand symphony of software operations. As we stand on the cusp of a container-driven future, mastering the intricacies of container management will be the distinguishing factor between cacophony and harmony in the software realm.

Docker Compose basics

In the expansive terrain of software development, Docker emerged as a beacon of consistency and portability, encapsulating applications within resilient containers. But as applications grew complex, the need to manage a plethora of interlinked containers arose. Introducing Docker Compose—a tool designed to knit together diverse containers into coherent, orchestrated systems. Delving into Docker Compose's fundamentals reveals its power, its elegance, and its indispensability in managing multi-container applications.

At its heart, Docker Compose is a tool for defining and managing multi-container Docker applications. Whereas Docker's primary role is to encapsulate individual applications within containers, Docker Compose extends this paradigm to whole ecosystems of interdependent containers. An e-commerce platform, for instance, requires a web server container, a database container, and another for caching. Running and interlinking these containers manually would be a tedious, error-prone endeavor. Docker Compose addresses this challenge by allowing developers to define, configure, and run such multi-container applications using a single, declarative file—the docker-compose.yml.

The docker-compose.yml file serves as the bedrock of any Docker Compose project. Within its confines, developers articulate the architecture of their application, specifying the containers required, their interrelations, volumes, networks, and more. Every service, representing a container, is defined with its image, environment variables, ports, and other configuration details. It's in this file that the magic of Docker Compose becomes palpable. With a simple textual representation, developers can delineate intricate application architectures, ensuring that every component, from databases to microservices, finds its place in the orchestration.

Once the blueprint in docker-compose.yml is established, bringing the application to life is a matter of a single command—docker-compose up. With this command, Docker Compose references the defined YAML file, creating, starting, and interlinking all specified containers. The resulting ecosystem is a harmonious interplay of containers, each performing its designated role, yet functioning as part of a cohesive whole. Conversely, tearing down such an orchestrated setup is equally streamlined with the docker-compose down command, ensuring that developers can effortlessly switch between environments, configurations, or application versions.

Docker Compose's utility continues beyond merely orchestration. As applications undergo development, testing, and scaling, their configurations often need tweaking. Docker Compose accommodates this dynamism, permitting developers to adjust container configurations, scale specific services, or even redefine networks—all without altering the underlying Docker images. With commands like docker-compose scale, developers can instantiate multiple instances of a specific service, facilitating load distribution and redundancy. This scalability, intrinsic to Docker Compose's design, ensures that applications remain agile, responsive, and resilient, regardless of user demands or external pressures.

A quintessential feature of Docker Compose, often overlooked, is its ability to facilitate local development. In traditional setups, replicating production environments on local machines was fraught with inconsistencies and discrepancies. Docker Compose, by encapsulating the entire application architecture within a declarative file, bridges this divide. Developers can instantiate entire application stacks on their local machines, mirroring production setups with unparalleled fidelity. This congruence between local and production environments accelerates development cycles, minimizes deployment anomalies, and fosters a culture of "develop once, run anywhere."

Yet, Docker Compose's brilliance isn't just in its capabilities—it's in its simplicity. For developers transitioning into the containerized world, Docker Compose offers a gentle learning curve. The YAML syntax, while powerful, is intuitive, making the process of defining complex architectures surprisingly straightforward. Moreover,

Docker Compose's tight integration with Docker ensures that developers can leverage their existing Docker knowledge, weaving it seamlessly into the realm of multi-container orchestration.

In conclusion, Docker Compose emerges as a pivotal tool in the modern developer's arsenal—a tool that transforms intricate application architectures into manageable, replicable, and scalable systems. As the world gravitates towards microservices and modular design, the ability to cohesively orchestrate disparate containers becomes imperative. Docker Compose, with its blend of simplicity and power, stands poised to shepherd this transition. It encapsulates the ethos of modern software development, emphasizing modularity, consistency, and agility. As applications evolve, branching into multifaceted ecosystems of interdependent services, Docker Compose ensures they do so harmoniously, orchestrating containerized symphonies with grace and precision. In the tapestry of containerization, Docker Compose is the thread that binds, the force that aligns, and the maestro that orchestrates.

CHAPTER IV

Creating Your First Dockerfile

Dockerfile structure

Amidst the vast and vibrant realm of containerization, Docker has firmly established its dominance, championing the virtues of consistency, portability, and scalability. At the crux of Docker's prowess lies its ability to encapsulate applications within containers, ensuring they function seamlessly across diverse environments. The blueprint guiding this encapsulation process is the Dockerfile—a meticulously structured document that instructs Docker on how to build an image, which subsequently serves as the foundation for a container. Unraveling the intricacies of Dockerfile's structure reveals the nuances, the thoughtfulness, and the strategic foresight embedded in Docker's design philosophy.

A Dockerfile, in its essence, is a script composed of various commands and arguments. Each command corresponds to a specific instruction, directing Docker to construct an image. Within these commands, the Dockerfile unveils its layered architecture, with each layer representing a distinct step in the image-building process. This layered approach isn't merely an architectural choice—it's a strategic decision, ensuring that Docker can leverage caching efficiently, thereby accelerating subsequent image builds.

The journey through a Dockerfile typically begins with the FROM command. This foundational directive specifies the base image upon which all subsequent modifications and installations will be layered. It's a pivotal decision influencing the image's size, security profile, and capabilities. Developers might choose official images of popular operating systems, like Ubuntu or Alpine, or opt for application-specific bases, such as Node or Python. The choice here embodies the balance between minimalism and functionality, with developers often seeking images that provide the requisite environment without extraneous bloat.

With the base image established, a Dockerfile delves into configuration and environment setup. Commands like LABEL allow developers to annotate their image with metadata, providing context, authorship details, or version information. Meanwhile, the ENV command defines environment variables, setting key-value pairs that might be pivotal for the application's runtime configuration.

But a Dockerfile's real magic starts unfolding as it begins to shape the environment. The RUN command, one of the most frequently used directives, executes shell commands within the current image layer. Through RUN, developers install software packages, set up directories, adjust permissions, and perform myriad other tasks. This command morphs the base image into an environment tailored to the application. Due to its significance, developers are often advised to use it judiciously, combining multiple operations within a single

RUN command where feasible, to minimize the creation of additional layers and optimize image size.

As the Dockerfile crafts the environment, it also ensures that the application's source code and assets find their way into the image. The COPY and ADD commands facilitate this transfer. While both commands serve to copy files or directories from the host into the image, ADD possesses additional capabilities, such as extracting tarball content or fetching remote URLs. In most scenarios, the simplicity and clarity of COPY make it the preferred choice, but ADD stands ready for more specialized tasks.

When instantiated, a Docker container's behavior is governed by its entry point and command—two directives specified using the ENTRYPOINT and CMD commands in the Dockerfile. While both can define the executable to run within the container, their flexibility and intent differ. ENTRYPOINT sets a fixed starting point, often a specific script or application, whereas CMD specifies the default arguments that can be overridden upon container instantiation. In tandem, these commands determine the container's primary function and behavior.

Yet, a Dockerfile's responsibilities aren't confined to the container's interior. Through commands like EXPOSE and VOLUME, it interacts with the broader ecosystem. EXPOSE informs Docker that the container will listen on specific network ports at runtime, facilitating communication with external entities. Conversely, VOLUME creates a mount point, allowing containers to share directories with the host system or other containers, ensuring data persistence and inter-container communication.

In conclusion, the Dockerfile is similar to an architect's blueprint, detailing each brick, beam, and bolt. Its structured format, evolving layer by layer, embodies the principles of clarity, modularity, and efficiency. By delineating each step, each modification, and each configuration with precision, the Dockerfile ensures that Docker images are replicable, consistent, and tailored to their intended purpose. As the world steers towards containerized infrastructures and microservices, the Dockerfile, with its intricate structure and strategic design, is a testament to the foresight and innovation embedded in Docker's DNA. It's the silent guardian, the meticulous craftsman, sculpting the vessels that power modern software landscapes.

Writing a basic Dockerfile

In the sprawling landscapes of modern software development, Docker has emerged as a luminary, casting a radiant glow of consistency and portability. Its promise to developers is compelling: "Code once, run anywhere." Yet, this promise is actualized not just by the Docker engine itself, but significantly by a humble script known as the Dockerfile. This text file, seemingly innocent, wields immense power, guiding Docker in its quest to encapsulate applications within pristine containers. Writing a basic Dockerfile is an exercise in precision, foresight, and understanding—a journey worth embarking upon for any software artisan.

Embarking on creating a Dockerfile begins with an elemental declaration: the FROM directive. This command is the foundation upon which the rest of the Dockerfile will stand. It informs Docker about the base image from which the building process will commence. This could be an official operating system image like Debian or Alpine for many applications. Alternatively, it could be an application-specific image, like Python or Node.js, which provides a predefined environment tailored for a particular programming language or tool. Thus, the FROM directive is more than just a starting point; it's a strategic choice, reflecting the developer's intentions about the environment in which the application will thrive.

With the foundation firmly set, the Dockerfile's next endeavor is to ensure that the application environment is sculpted to perfection. This task falls upon the shoulders of the RUN directive. A powerful command, RUN, facilitates the execution of shell commands within the context of the image. It's through a series of RUN instructions that a developer installs essential software packages, creates necessary directories, or sets appropriate permissions. Each RUN instruction adds a new layer to the Docker image, capturing the modifications made. Hence, it's a practice of prudence to group related commands under a single RUN to ensure the final image remains sleek and optimized.

However, no matter how refined, an environment is inert without the application it's meant to support. Thus, the Dockerfile incorporates the application's source code and related assets. Two directives rise to this occasion: COPY and ADD. Both transport files or directories from the host system into the image. While their purpose overlaps, their capabilities differ subtly. COPY offers a straightforward file copying mechanism, while ADD comes with additional talents, such as remote URL support and automatic tarball extraction. For most Dockerfile authors, COPY becomes the go-to command due to its clarity and simplicity.

Beyond just embedding the application, a Dockerfile must also delineate how the application should behave within the container. This behavior is often orchestrated through two interlinked directives: CMD and ENTRYPOINT. While both can influence the executable that runs when a container starts, they serve nuanced roles. The ENTRYPOINT provides a fixed starting point for the container, perhaps a specific script or binary. Meanwhile, CMD specifies default arguments that can be passed to the entry point, arguments that can be overridden when the container is launched. Together, they shape the container's primary function, determining what it does when it springs to life.

No application, however, operates in isolation. It communicates, it interacts, and it shares. Recognizing this, the Dockerfile provides directives facilitating interactions between the container and the external world. The EXPOSE command signifies the network ports the container will utilize, ensuring other entities can communicate with the application housed within. Similarly, the VOLUME directive creates designated mount points, enabling containers to interface with the host system or other containers, a mechanism especially vital for data persistence or shared configurations.

Writing a basic Dockerfile, thus, is an exercise in sequential artistry. Each directive, each command, is like a brushstroke, shaping the canvas of the container environment. Yet, writing a Dockerfile transcends mere syntax; it's an exploration of the application's soul, understanding its needs, behaviors, and interactions. A well-crafted Dockerfile ensures that the application runs and thrives, benefiting from the consistency and isolation Docker promises.

In conclusion, the Dockerfile is an emblem of Docker's philosophy—a philosophy that champions reproducibility, portability, and scalability. Writing a Dockerfile is both a science and an art, demanding technical understanding and a deep appreciation of the application's essence. As more developers embrace the world of containerization, mastering the art of Dockerfile creation becomes not just a desirable skill but a quintessential one. Through these carefully crafted scripts, applications embark on their journey, sailing the seas of diverse environments, yet always finding familiar shores, thanks to the guiding light of Docker.

Building an image from a Dockerfile

Docker has risen as a beacon of portability, innovation, and efficiency in the software development universe. Its prominence hinges on its unique capability to house applications within containers, ensuring they function consistently across various environments. At the epicenter of this capability is the Dockerfile— a comprehensive script detailing the assembly process of a Docker container. Yet, the Dockerfile, with all its meticulous instructions, remains a mere blueprint until it undergoes the transformative process of building. During this build process, the Dockerfile's textual guidelines metamorphose into a tangible Docker image, ready to breathe life into containers. Understanding this process is pivotal for developers navigating the containerized waters of modern software infrastructure.

To begin with, building an image from a Dockerfile is orchestrated by Docker's build engine—a sophisticated system designed to parse, interpret, and execute the Dockerfile's instructions sequentially. The command docker build triggers the initiation of this process. At its core, this command is deceptively simple, but underneath, it sets into motion a cascade of events that bring the Dockerfile to life.

Once triggered, Docker's build engine takes the helm, starting its journey with the first line of the Dockerfile. Typically, this line encapsulates the FROM directive, instructing the engine about the base image that should be fetched. Depending on the specified image, Docker reaches out to a repository (often Docker Hub, unless a different registry is mentioned) to retrieve it. This base image forms the foundational layer upon which all subsequent modifications, dictated by the Dockerfile, will be layered.

Each successive instruction in the Dockerfile then prompts Docker to create a new layer atop the preceding one. Layers are, in essence, the bedrock of Docker's efficiency, allowing the system to cache results and expedite rebuilds when only a part of the Dockerfile changes. For instance, if a Dockerfile instruction involves installing a software package and that instruction hasn't changed between builds, Docker can reuse the cached layer, bypassing the need for a fresh installation.

However, during the interpretation of the RUN instructions, the build process truly showcases its prowess. These commands, which might involve installing additional packages, modifying file permissions, or setting up configurations, are executed in an intermediary container spun up from the current image state. Once the command concludes its operation, the resultant changes are committed to a new layer, and the intermediary container is gracefully discarded. This step-by-step, containerized approach ensures precision, allowing the build engine to capture the exact changes corresponding to each Dockerfile instruction.

Incorporating the application's actual code or assets into the image often involves COPY or ADD directives. When the build engine encounters these instructions, it transfers the specified files or directories from the host system into the image. Herein lies a crucial distinction between building and runtime. While the application code gets embedded within the image during the build process, it's only within an instantiated container that the code actively executes during runtime.

As the build process progresses, interpreting each Dockerfile directive, it meticulously crafts the environment, sets configurations, and embeds assets. Yet, the CMD and ENTRYPOINT directives truly define the image's purpose, signifying what action the container should undertake upon instantiation. These directives, once processed, don't actively change the image's filesystem; instead, they set metadata that influences the container's behavior during its runtime.

The culmination of the build process is marked by Docker packaging all the processed layers into a cohesive Docker image. This image, now a tangible artifact, is stored locally within the Docker host's image repository. Post-build, developers often assign a tag to this image using the -t option, which aids in versioning and organizing images. This tagging mechanism ensures that images can be effectively managed, retrieved, and deployed, especially in scenarios where iterative development leads to multiple image versions.

Reflecting upon this journey, building an image from a Dockerfile stands as a testament to Docker's genius. It's a dance of precision, where textual directives are methodically translated into tangible changes, layer by layer. Each step, from fetching the base image to embedding application assets, is executed with an acute attention to detail, ensuring the resultant image manifests the Dockerfile's intent.

In conclusion, building a Docker image from a Dockerfile is much more than a mere technical process; it's an alchemy where code, configuration, and content merge to form a singular entity ready for deployment. For developers, understanding this build process isn't just a matter of curiosity; it's a gateway to harnessing Docker's full potential, ensuring that applications are not just containerized but are containerized with clarity, efficiency, and purpose.

CHAPTER V

Container Management

Starting, stopping, and restarting containers

The realm of containerization, spearheaded by Docker, has revolutionized the software landscape, offering a harmonious blend of flexibility, consistency, and efficiency. As developers and system administrators dive deep into this world, they are often met with the fundamental aspects of container lifecycle management—starting, stopping, and restarting. Like a symphony with its crescendos, diminuendos, and resounding climaxes, managing a container's lifecycle requires rhythm and finesse, ensuring applications housed within these containers deliver optimal performance, reliability, and responsiveness.

Initiating a container is akin to igniting a spark that brings a lifeless entity into bustling existence. The magic of this transformation is embodied in the docker start command. However, before one can even harness this command, a container must first be created, typically achieved using docker create paired with an image of choice. This creation process molds an inert container, primed and ready, but not yet active. With the docker start command, this dormant container awakens, instantiating the processes defined within the image, often as directed by the CMD or ENTRYPOINT instructions of its originating Dockerfile. This transition from a passive state to an active one is significant, as it not only marks the commencement of application operations but also signals Docker's under-the-hood orchestration—allocating resources, establishing network connections, and ensuring isolation.

However, the software world is dynamic, with ever-changing requirements, sporadic surges in demands, or routine maintenance needs. Such scenarios often necessitate halting a container, a task realized through the docker stop command. Stopping a container is not an abrupt termination but rather a graceful conclusion, allowing processes within the container a window of time to finish ongoing tasks and shut down properly. Underlying this command is a two-fold mechanism. Initially, a SIGTERM signal is dispatched to the primary process within the container, urging it to conclude. If the process lingers after a stipulated interval, a more forceful SIGKILL signal intervenes, ensuring the container's termination. Docker strives to balance urgency with grace through this phased approach, ensuring operations are halted without unnecessary disruptions.

Yet, in the intricate dance of software operations, there are moments when a mere cessation isn't sufficient; a revival is desired. These are instances where configurations might be tweaked, patches applied, or resources adjusted, mandating a stop and a subsequent start. In its wisdom, Docker offers a streamlined solution in the guise of the docker restart command. This command, though simple in its invocation, encapsulates the dual actions of stopping and immediately starting a container. It offers developers and administrators a swift route to rejuvenate a container, ensuring minimal downtime and a seamless transition from one operational state to another.

The act of managing a container's lifecycle, though primarily centered around these commands, is augmented by other Docker utilities. For instance, the docker pause command allows one to temporarily halt a container's processes without actually stopping the container, akin to pressing a 'pause' button. When operations need to resume, docker unpause seamlessly reintroduces the halted processes. Furthermore, for those curious about the state of a container—whether it's running, stopped, or paused—the docker inspect command offers a deep dive, providing granular details about the container's current status and configuration.

Reflecting on this lifecycle management, one might draw parallels to the rhythms of nature—the dawn marking a start, the dusk signaling a stop, and the cycles of the moon symbolizing the repeated restarts. However, beyond this poetic semblance lies a world of technical precision, where these commands play pivotal roles in ensuring software reliability, performance optimization, and resource efficiency. A stopped container, for instance, conserves system resources, freeing them for other tasks. Conversely, a restarted container might be a gateway to harnessing updated configurations or freshly released features.

In essence, the capabilities to start, stop, and restart containers aren't just mechanical operations within Docker; they are the heartbeats of the containerized ecosystem. They signify the fluidity and flexibility that Docker brings to the software world, allowing applications to adapt, evolve, and respond to the diverse and dynamic demands of modern computing environments.

In conclusion, as Docker continues to solidify its stature in the software arena, a profound understanding of container lifecycle management becomes imperative. Starting, stopping, and restarting containers isn't a mere trio of commands; it's a symphony of orchestrated operations, ensuring that applications, though housed in ephemeral containers, deliver lasting impacts.

Monitoring and logging

Docker containers have emerged as celestial bodies of consistency and portability in the vast expanse of the software cosmos. They carry the precious cargo of applications within their encapsulated environments, running them seamlessly across varying infrastructures. However, as astronomers need telescopes to study distant stars, software developers and system administrators require tools and methodologies to keep a vigilant eye on these containers. Encapsulated in monitoring and logging, this observational process becomes the linchpin for ensuring containerized applications' health, performance, and reliability.

Monitoring in the context of containers is the continuous process of gathering metrics and data points about the container's operational state. It's akin to a medical checkup, where vital signs like heart rate or blood pressure are gauged. In the container world, these "vital signs" span a range of metrics like CPU usage, memory consumption, network activity, and disk I/O. Monitoring provides an overarching view of the container's health, enabling developers to assess whether the container and its encapsulated application are performing optimally or if they are under duress, possibly hinting at underlying issues.

Docker, in its inherent design, offers rudimentary tools for monitoring. The docker stats command, for instance, provides real-time statistics about running containers, detailing their CPU, memory, and network usage. While this offers a snapshot view, it's often insufficient for comprehensive, long-term observation. Recognizing this gap, many third-party solutions have burgeoned in the ecosystem. Tools like Prometheus, paired with Grafana for visualization, or cAdvisor, crafted explicitly for container monitoring, empower developers with deeper insights. These tools accumulate and visualize metrics and allow for setting alerts, ensuring that anomalous behavior or resource thresholds trigger timely notifications.

Yet, while monitoring provides a holistic overview, the granular details often pinpoint specific issues or anomalies. This is where logging comes into play, acting as the detailed chronicles of a container's life. Logging captures discrete events or messages generated by the application or system processes within the container. Each log entry, stamped with a timestamp, narrates a story—a user's access, an error during data processing, or even routine status updates.

Docker, aware of the importance of logs, integrates a logging mechanism natively. The docker logs command allows users to fetch and tail the logs of a specific container, typically capturing the stdout and stderr outputs of the container's primary process. However, in large-scale deployments or intricate microservices architectures, relying solely on Docker's native logging can become cumbersome. Logs from myriad containers can become a veritable haystack, making the task of pinpointing specific log entries analogous to finding a needle.

This challenge has fueled the rise of specialized logging solutions tailored for the containerized world. Tools like ELK Stack (Elasticsearch, Logstash, and Kibana) or Loki provide centralized logging platforms. These tools aggregate logs from various containers, offering powerful search capabilities, advanced filtering, and intuitive visualization. Furthermore, they often integrate seamlessly with monitoring solutions, presenting a unified dashboard where metrics and logs merge, offering a bird's-eye view and granular insights.

However, monitoring and logging isn't solely about gathering data but deriving actionable insights. A sudden spike in CPU usage, combined with logs detailing database access errors, might hint at a faulty query causing undue stress on the system. Conversely, an uptick in memory consumption, coinciding with logs indicating high user traffic, might suggest scaling up resources or optimizing application processes.

In conclusion, monitoring and logging in Docker containers aren't merely observational processes; they are the critical feedback loops ensuring the resilience and efficiency of containerized applications.

They act as the watchful eyes, always scanning the horizons for signs of trouble, and the attentive ears, attuned to the myriad stories whispered by logs. For developers and system administrators, mastering these domains isn't just a luxury—it's an imperative. In the ever-evolving software world, where change is the only constant, monitoring and logging stand as steadfast sentinels, guarding against disruptions, ensuring continuity, and driving optimization.

Networking and communication between containers

In the intricate tapestry of modern software, containers represent individual threads, each vibrant with its color and purpose. While they shine in their solitary capacities, their interplay, the patterns they form when woven together, crafts the broader narrative of applications. This interplay, founded on networking and communication, is the lifeblood of microservices architectures, where containers often run interdependent services that must collaborate seamlessly. However, enabling this seemingly simple act of communication is a maze of protocols, technologies, and configurations. Navigating this maze requires understanding Docker's sophisticated approach to networking and the mechanisms it uses to facilitate container-to-container discourse.

The notion of network drivers is at the heart of Docker's networking philosophy. Much like a country with its highways, railways, and air routes, Docker offers multiple avenues for communication, each with its distinct characteristics. The default network driver, known as the 'bridge,' is akin to a country's internal road network. Containers connected to a bridge network can communicate freely, yet they remain insulated from the host, using a private internal IP range. This seclusion offers a layer of security, ensuring that the containerized applications are shielded from external threats.

However, there are instances where a container needs to be more accessible, to perhaps serve a web application or listen to incoming database requests. Here, Docker's 'host' network comes into play, aligning the container's network stack directly with the host. While offering performance advantages and simpler addressability, such a configuration does expose the container to the broader network, a trade-off that developers must consider based on the application's needs.

In more complex scenarios, where containers sprawl across multiple hosts or must be organized in distinct communication groups, Docker's 'overlay' and 'macvlan' networks emerge as solutions. Like an international flight network, the overlay network connects containers across different Docker daemon hosts, bridging them via encrypted tunnels. This setup is particularly valuable in Docker Swarm configurations, where services may be distributed across a cluster. On the other hand, the 'macvlan' network assigns a unique MAC address to containers, allowing them to appear as physical devices on the network, easing communication with enterprise systems or legacy applications that rely on MAC address-based configurations.

With the foundational networks established, service discovery and name resolution are the next pivotal consideration. In a world where containers can be dynamically created or destroyed, relying on static

IP addresses is impractical. Docker addresses this challenge by integrating an embedded DNS server, allowing containers to communicate using container names instead of volatile IPs. This abstraction simplifies inter-container discourse and offers a level of decoupling, where services can be scaled, migrated, or updated without disrupting the communication fabric.

Yet, networking doesn't end with just establishing connections; it extends to managing data traffic, ensuring efficient load distribution, and safeguarding against failures. Docker's native load balancing mechanisms kick in here, mainly when operating in Swarm mode. Incoming requests to a service are smartly routed to individual containers, ensuring that no single container is overwhelmed while others remain idle. This load distribution not only optimizes resource utilization but also enhances application responsiveness.

However, the realm of container networking isn't devoid of challenges. Network latency, data bottlenecks, and security vulnerabilities can be potential pitfalls. Addressing these requires a blend of best practices, such as minimizing inter-service calls, ensuring proper encapsulation and isolation, and regularly auditing and updating container images and configurations to guard against security loopholes.

In conclusion, enabling communication between Docker containers is a journey through a sophisticated landscape of networks, protocols, and configurations. While the underlying complexities can be daunting, Docker strives to make this journey smoother for developers and system administrators with its intuitive defaults and extensible drivers. As containerized applications grow in scale and intricacy, mastering this networking domain becomes beneficial and essential. For, in the grand orchestra of software, each container, like an individual instrument, needs to be in perfect tune, but it's their collective symphony, enabled by flawless communication, that leaves an indelible impact.

CHAPTER VI

Docker Volumes
and Data Persistence

What are Docker volumes?

In the dynamic realm of containerization, where ephemeral instances rise and dissolve with rhythmic regularity, the question of persistence lingers with profound resonance. Containers, by their very design, are transient entities. They are birthed from images, execute their duties, and eventually evaporate, leaving no trace of their brief existence behind. Yet, within the realm of software, not everything is fleeting. Data, configurations, logs are the lasting artifacts that applications produce and consume. Ensuring their persistence, their continuity across container lifecycles, becomes a paramount concern. Introducing Docker volumes, the guardians of persistence, acting as the bridge between the transient world of containers and the enduring universe of data.

Docker volumes can be imagined as sanctuaries, distinct regions in the host's filesystem, where data can reside safely, shielded from the capricious lifecycle of the container. When a container writes data, it typically does so within its writable layer, a thin veneer atop its underlying image. This data, while accessible during the container's lifespan, vanishes with its cessation. However, containers can redirect their data operations to these external sanctuaries by leveraging volumes. As a result, even when containers fade, the data within these volumes endures, available for subsequent containers or external processes to access and manipulate.

But why is such persistence essential? Consider the example of a database container. By their very nature, databases are accumulators of state, growing repositories of information that applications and users feed into. If this state were to reside solely within the container's writable layer, every cessation, be it intentional or accidental, would result in data loss, rendering the database ineffective. By employing Docker volumes, databases can ensure that their accumulated state remains intact, ready to be accessed by subsequent container incarnations or even different services.

Docker's approach to volumes isn't monolithic; it's nuanced, offering varied modes of operation to cater to different needs. At its simplest, the bind mount links a specific directory on the host directly to the container. This approach offers a straightforward mapping, making it apt for scenarios where particular locations on the host need to be accessible within the container, like configuration files or local development setups. However, this direct linkage also implies a tight coupling between the host and container filesystems, requiring precise path specifications.

To provide a more abstracted, managed form of persistence, Docker introduced named volumes. These are volumes that Docker itself manages, storing them in a designated part of the host's filesystem, typically under /var/lib/docker/volumes. When creating a named volume, users don't need to fret about specific paths; they simply provide a name, and Docker handles the underlying storage. This abstraction not only simplifies volume management but also ensures a level of isolation, minimizing potential conflicts or overlaps.

Beyond these native mechanisms, Docker also supports volume plugins, extending its storage capabilities to external platforms or solutions. Whether cloud storage services like AWS EBS or specialized filesystems like GlusterFS, volume plugins enable Docker to integrate seamlessly with these platforms, offering enhanced scalability, redundancy, or performance characteristics.

The utility of Docker volumes, however, extends beyond just persistence. They also play pivotal roles in data sharing and migration. Multiple containers can concurrently access a single volume, facilitating real-time data exchange. This capability becomes invaluable in patterns like the sidecar design, where one container might produce data while another processes or transmits it. Furthermore, volumes can be backed up, cloned, or transferred, enabling data mobility across hosts, environments, or even geographic regions.

Yet, as with all powerful tools, Docker volumes come with their considerations. Ensuring data consistency, especially in concurrent access scenarios, requires mechanisms like locking or careful orchestration. Security, too, emerges as a concern. Since volumes can persist sensitive data, measures like encryption, access controls, and regular audits become imperative to guard against potential breaches or misuse.

In conclusion, Docker volumes stand as sentinel towers in the ever-shifting sands of containerization. They offer a vantage point from where data, in all its gravity, remains anchored, undisturbed by the swirling winds of container lifecycles. For developers and system administrators, understanding and mastering volumes isn't just a technical endeavor; it's a commitment to ensuring that amidst the fleeting choreography of containers, the essential pulse of data never skips a beat.

Creating and managing volumes

In the expansive realm of container orchestration, tension exists between the ephemeral and the enduring. While containers, by design, thrive on transience, some aspects of applications demand constancy. With its intrinsic value, data is often the cornerstone of this persistent universe. Addressing the dichotomy between containers' fleeting life and data's enduring nature, Docker volumes emerge as a harmonizing solution. These storage entities, decoupled from the evanescent lifecycle of containers, become vital repositories where data remains anchored. However, the mere existence of such a mechanism isn't sufficient. The true mastery lies in creating, managing, and optimizing these volumes, ensuring that they effectively serve the needs of both the data and the applications that rely upon it.

Creating a Docker volume can be visualized as setting up a sanctuary for data. With a simple command, docker volume create, Docker carves out a designated space within the host's filesystem. This space, abstracted from the users by Docker, becomes the sanctified ground where data can reside safely, immune to the tumultuous life of containers. For users who desire more control or specificity, Docker can specify storage options, paths, or even integrate with external storage platforms using volume drivers. The versatility of this creation process, from its stark simplicity to its granular control, mirrors the diverse needs of applications, ranging from rudimentary logs to intricate databases.

However, creation is merely the genesis. The real challenge, and perhaps the essence of volume management, lies in the subsequent stages. Associating volumes with containers becomes the immediate following task. Volumes can be tethered to containers through the --mount flag during container initiation, creating a conduit for data exchange. This association isn't just a static link; it's an active channel that facilitates reading and writing data, ensuring that the container can seamlessly interact with its persistent storage counterpart.

Beyond mere association, the management of volumes delves into deeper intricacies. Inspecting volumes, for instance, becomes essential to understand their properties, configurations, or utilization. The docker volume inspect command unfurls a detailed blueprint of the volume, revealing its path, driver, options, and other metadata. Such insights assist in troubleshooting and capacity planning, ensuring that volumes are optimally utilized and aren't burgeoning or depleting unexpectedly.

However, the life of a volume isn't eternally bound to its originating host or environment. Migration, backup, and restoration are pivotal tasks in the volume management odyssey. Using mechanisms like docker volume cp or integrating with backup solutions, volumes can be archived, cloned, or shifted, ensuring data mobility and resilience. Whether it's migrating data to a more potent host, creating redundancies across geographic regions, or simply preserving data for posterity, these operations amplify the value of volumes, elevating them from mere storage entities to strategic assets.

Yet, even in persistent storage, not all volumes are destined for perpetuity. Pruning and deletion become necessary rituals in the lifecycle of volumes. Over time, as containers perish and applications evolve, specific volumes may become orphaned or redundant. Retaining such vestigial volumes consumes precious storage resources and introduces clutter, complicating management tasks. Docker's docker volume rm and docker volume prune command step in here, enabling users to surgically remove specific volumes or cleanse the system of all unused volumes, respectively.

However, the act of volume management isn't devoid of pitfalls. The concurrency of access, especially in environments where multiple containers interact with a single volume, introduces potential issues of data consistency and corruption. Here, strategies like locking, transactional operations, or careful orchestration become paramount. Security, too, looms as a looming concern. Given that volumes may store sensitive information, it becomes imperative to implement encryption, access controls, and regular audits.

In conclusion, Docker volumes, in their essence, are the answer to a profound dilemma within containerization: how to ensure data's longevity amidst a sea of transience. While the mechanisms to create and manage them might seem technical, they're rooted in deeper philosophical concerns about data's value, continuity, and safety. For developers and system administrators, mastering the art of volume management isn't just a technical endeavor; it's a journey that ensures that amidst the orchestrated dance of containers, the silent rhythm of data remains unbroken.

Backup and restore strategies

In the ephemeral dance of containers, where instances flicker in and out of existence in orchestrated harmony, Docker volumes serve as the continuous heartbeat, preserving the lifeblood of applications: data. As invaluable as data is, preserving it in a running environment isn't sufficient. Ensuring its resilience, safeguarding it against failures, mishaps, or calamities, becomes a paramount concern. Addressing this concern are backup and restore strategies tailored for Docker volumes, which stand as sentinels, ensuring that data's vitality remains uncompromised across scenarios and timeframes.

The very essence of backing up data can be likened to creating reflections of reality. Frozen in time, these reflections can be revisited, reconstructed, or even transitioned across environments. In its inherent design, Docker does not include built-in backup mechanisms for volumes. However, the architectural flexibility of Docker and the universality of its volumes ensure that traditional backup tools and practices can be seamlessly integrated, with some adaptations, to cater to containerized environments.

To understand backup strategies, one must first grasp the physicality of Docker volumes. Docker volumes reside on the host's filesystem, usually within the path /var/lib/docker/volumes. Recognizing this storage layout becomes the first step in designing backup approaches. Basic backup strategies often employ traditional tools like tar or rsync to archive the contents of these volumes. For instance, using a simple tar command, the contents of a volume can be bundled into an archive, which can then be stored in backup repositories or even offsite locations.

However, while basic file-based backups cater to a wide array of scenarios, they might not suffice for more intricate applications, especially databases. With their transactional nature, continuous writes, and complex data structures, databases pose unique challenges. Here, application-consistent backups emerge as a necessity. Such backups, often facilitated by database-native tools, ensure the data's state is coherent, consistent, and devoid of corruption or partial writes. Integrating such tools with Docker often entails running backup operations within containers themselves or utilizing database replication mechanisms to offload backup tasks to replica instances, minimizing the impact on primary operations.

Beyond mere data backup, metadata and configuration about Docker volumes also warrant preservation. Capturing volume configurations, mount points, drivers, and other metadata ensures that backups are not just data-dumps but holistic snapshots, ready for seamless restoration. Tools like docker volume inspect can be leveraged to extract and archive this metadata alongside the data backups.

As pivotal as backups are, their true value is realized only when paired with robust restoration strategies. Restoration is more than just data retrieval; it revives applications, resurrects their state, and ensures continuity. Basic restorations, especially for file-based backups, involve simply extracting archived contents back to Docker volume paths. However, the complexity scales with the intricacy of applications. Restoring databases, for instance, might involve not just data restoration but also replaying transaction logs, ensuring data integrity, and validating schemas. Additionally, when restoring from application-consistent backups, it becomes essential to ensure that the Docker environment mirrors the original, especially regarding network configurations, dependencies, and linked services.

While backup and restore operations are twin pillars of data resilience, their effectiveness is contingent upon regular testing and validation. Backup validation, involving periodic restoration in isolated environments, ensures that backups are complete and coherent. Such tests safeguard against silent corruptions, missed files, or misconfigurations that might creep into backup routines.

Yet, as robust as backup and restore strategies might be, they aren't devoid of challenges. Data gravity, especially in environments with voluminous data, can impede backup speeds, necessitating strategies like differential or incremental backups. Ensuring backup security, given data sensitivity, demands encryption, both at rest and in transit.

Moreover, backup storage considerations— scalability, redundancy, and cost—also play pivotal roles in shaping backup strategies.

In conclusion, Docker volumes, while serving as reservoirs of persistent data, demand strategies that transcend mere storage. Backup and restore operations, in this context, emerge as vital lifelines, ensuring that data remains indomitable, resilient to failures, and ever-ready for revival. For those navigating the containerized landscapes of modern applications, mastering these strategies isn't just a technical pursuit; it's an affirmation of the sanctity of data, a commitment to preserving its essence across time and turmoil.

CHAPTER VII

Docker Networking

Basics of Docker networking

In the intricate world of software orchestration, where isolated units of applications, known as containers, dynamically spring to life and cease, communication is the very lifeblood that sustains their operations. These ephemeral entities, running distinct fragments of applications, often require intricate choreography to interact with each other, external systems, or even the users they serve. Facilitating this ballet of bytes is Docker's networking system, an understated yet profoundly crucial component of containerized architectures.

To comprehend the nuances of Docker networking, one must first understand its raison d'être. Containers, by their inherent nature, are isolated. While being a boon for consistency, reproducibility, and security, this isolation also poses challenges when it comes to inter-container communication or external access. Docker's networking framework emerges as a bridge, transcending these isolation barriers, and enabling containers to function not as secluded islands, but as interconnected nodes in a larger ecosystem.

At the heart of Docker's networking model are networks. Conceptually abstract yet operationally pivotal, these networks serve as virtual fabrics upon which containers can be tethered. In its wisdom, Docker provides several out-of-the-box network drivers, each tailored for specific scenarios. The default drivers include bridge, host, overlay, and macvlan. The bridge network, often the default for single-host setups, provides private internal IP addresses to containers, allowing them to communicate while isolating them from the external environment. For scenarios requiring containers to forgo any form of network isolation and share the host's network stack, the host network becomes the preferred choice. Multi-host scenarios, particularly prevalent in cluster orchestrations like Docker Swarm, necessitate the overlay network, enabling containers across different hosts to communicate as if they were on a singular, unified network. Lastly, the macvlan driver allows containers to be assigned MAC addresses, ensuring seamless integration with enterprise networks.

Creating and managing these networks is a task of profound simplicity, achieved through Docker's CLI. For instance, the docker network creates command, allowing users to instantiate networks, specifying the desired driver and other configuration parameters. Once created, containers can be effortlessly connected or disconnected from these networks, ensuring dynamic adaptability to application requirements.

Yet, the mere act of connecting containers to networks doesn't complete the networking narrative. Addressing—assigning IP addresses to containers—becomes an essential subtext of this story.

In its endeavor to abstract complexities, Docker provides an internal DNS server. Working with networks, this server ensures that containers can seamlessly resolve and communicate using container names, abstracting away the intricacies of IP address management.

However, facilitating inter-container communication is just one facet of Docker's networking prowess. Exposing containers to external entities—be it systems or users—demands port mapping. This operation, often realized through the -p flag during container instantiation, allows specific ports within containers to be mapped to ports on the host. Such a mechanism ensures that external entities can communicate with containerized applications by accessing mapped ports on the host, which then route the communication internally to the specified container ports.

Beyond the basics, Docker's networking landscape offers advanced features tailored to specific needs. Custom IPAM (IP Address Management) drivers allow for granular control over IP address assignments, catering to scenarios with bespoke addressing requirements. Network plugins, often third-party extensions, enable the integration of Docker's networking with external systems, providing solutions for specialized networking challenges or optimizations.

In its entirety, Docker's networking system, while seemingly complex, is anchored in intuitive principles. At its core, it endeavors to provide containers with the ability to communicate, interact, and serve, transcending their inherent isolation. It's a dance of bytes and packets, orchestrated with precision, ensuring that in the vast universe of containerized applications, no entity remains an isolated silo.

In conclusion, as Docker continues to redefine the paradigms of application deployment and orchestration, its networking subsystem stands as a testament to the intricate art of connecting the dots. For developers and system architects, understanding the basics of Docker networking isn't just a technical prerequisite; it's a journey into the heart of interconnected software ecosystems, where every byte, every packet, and every container tells a story of seamless collaboration in the vast tapestry of modern software landscapes.

Creating custom networks

In the rich tapestry of containerized environments, where isolated units of functionality, known as containers, operate, the essence of any productive orchestration lies in seamless interaction. Docker, the pioneer of modern containerization, recognizes this vital requirement and offers a networking solution and a flexible, adaptable framework wherein users can tailor-make their own communication channels. While deep-rooted in technicalities, this world of custom networks is an exercise in bridging isolated computational entities, painting a canvas of communication tailored for specific application landscapes.

To appreciate the need for custom networks, it's essential first to understand the default networking options Docker provides. Out-of-the-box, Docker offers network drivers such as bridge, host, and overlay, each designed for general scenarios, from single-host setups to multi-host orchestration. However, the default solutions may fall short as applications grow in complexity, encompassing multi-tier architectures, or when specific networking configurations become necessary due to security or performance reasons. In these nuanced terrains, custom networks emerge as the solution, offering a tailored communication path attuned to the unique requirements of specific applications.

Creating a custom network in Docker is anchored in its command-line interface. While the act might seem straightforward, the underlying decision-making requires a deep understanding of the application's architecture and its networking needs. When one uses the docker network create command, they're essentially crafting a new communication channel, a decision that comes with its own set of considerations. For instance, choosing a network driver is pivotal. Should containers communicate within a single host (bridge), or is there a requirement for inter-host communication (overlay)? Understanding the environment and scale at which the application operates is crucial to making this choice.

Another profound aspect of custom network creation is IP address management. Docker, by default, offers automatic IP assignment, abstracting away the complexities of IP management. However, with custom networks, specific IP ranges or subnets are often needed, especially when integrating with existing network architectures or when segregating application tiers. Here, the --subnet option during network creation allows users to specify a particular IP range, granting granular control over IP assignments. Similarly, the --gateway option can be employed to define a custom gateway for the network.

However, IP management isn't just about assignment; it's also about resolution. One of the unsung heroes in Docker's networking ecosystem is its internal DNS. By default, this DNS allows containers within a custom network to seamlessly communicate using container names, an abstraction that elevates user experience by negating the need to remember or manage IP addresses. While often taken for granted, this feature becomes crucial in dynamic environments where containers are frequently created or destroyed, ensuring that application components can consistently discover and communicate with each other.

Beyond these fundamental considerations, creating custom networks also comes with advanced options tailored for nuanced requirements. For instance, the --internal flag can create a network with no external access, ensuring that containers connected to this network remain isolated from external systems—a feature especially useful for sensitive application components or data. Similarly, for applications demanding network-level security, the --opt encrypted flag ensures that network traffic between containers is encrypted, bolstering data confidentiality and integrity.

While creating custom networks offers many options and flexibility, it's essential to approach it with a design mindset. What is the application's architecture? How do different components interact? Are there any specific security or performance considerations? Answering these questions becomes the foundation upon which custom networks should be built. It's a process that mirrors city planning, where roads (networks) are laid out based on current requirements and with a vision for future expansion, scalability, and adaptability.

In conclusion, the realm of Docker's custom networks is a testament to the flexibility and adaptability of containerized ecosystems. It recognizes that while containers are atomic units of computation, their true potential is realized only when they can interact, share, and collaborate. In this context, crafting custom networks is similar to sculpting an application's veins and arteries, ensuring the lifeblood of data flows seamlessly, efficiently, and securely. For developers and architects navigating the world of Docker, mastering the art of creating custom networks isn't just a technical pursuit; it's an embrace of the intricate choreography of modern applications, a dance of data on a canvas of custom communication channels.

Communication between containers on different networks

The need for communication reigns supreme in the expansive universe of container orchestration. It's one thing for containers on a singular network to interact, but the scenario becomes considerably more intricate when these containers sprawl across different networks. Docker, a cornerstone in container technology, offers not just a mechanism for such interspersed communication but also provides a sophisticated, flexible model that caters to the complexity and diversity of modern applications. Understanding how containers on disparate networks communicate is crucial, as it opens up avenues for design patterns that are both scalable and modular.

The principle underlying Docker's networking philosophy is one of isolation. Each network in Docker acts as a distinct entity, effectively isolating containers connected to it from those on other networks. At a primary glance, this might seem counterproductive—after all, isn't communication the end goal? However, this default behavior serves a critical purpose: establishing security boundaries, ensuring clean segregation of application tiers, and offering performance optimizations. But as with any principle, there are exceptions. In the vast expanse of application architectures, scenarios often arise where containers on different networks must converse. Docker, in its forward-thinking design, offers mechanisms to bridge this chasm.

To understand inter-network container communication, one must first delve into the essence of Docker's networking model. A network driver underpins each Docker network, and it's this driver that determines the network's behavior. The default bridge network, for instance, encapsulates containers within a private internal network on the host system, isolating them from both external systems and containers on other Docker networks. This inherent isolation can pose a challenge when inter-network communication is required.

However, Docker's flexibility comes to the fore in its link feature, an older mechanism which, while now considered legacy, was initially designed to facilitate communication between containers across separate networks. By explicitly linking containers, Docker set up environment variables and updated the /etc/hosts file to ensure containers were aware of each other, allowing them to communicate.

Yet, as Docker evolved, so did its networking capabilities. The link feature made way for user-defined bridge networks. Unlike the default bridge network, user-defined bridges allow automatic DNS resolution between containers, meaning containers on different user-defined bridge networks can communicate using their names. This provides an elegant solution to the interspersed communication problem, rendering the legacy link system obsolete in many scenarios.

But the tale of inter-network communication doesn't end with user-defined bridges. The overlay network, a driver tailored for Docker Swarm, Docker's native clustering system, elevates this narrative. Designed for multi-host communication, the overlay network ensures containers spanning multiple hosts—and inherently, multiple networks—can seamlessly communicate as if they were on a single unified network. This ensures a fluid data flow in clustered, distributed applications, abstracting away the underlying complexities of inter-host networking.

Yet, while Docker provides these tools, using them effectively requires architectural diligence. Care must be taken to ensure that communication across networks doesn't inadvertently expose sensitive components or create data bottlenecks. It's a balancing act, where the need for communication must be weighed against security, performance, and architectural clarity.

Moreover, as applications scale and evolve, so does their networking complexity. It's not uncommon for large-scale applications to comprise multiple networks, each catering to a specific application tier or module. In such scenarios, managing inter-network communication transitions from a technical task to an architectural endeavor. Decisions about which containers should communicate, the data they exchange, and the protocols they employ become pivotal, impacting not just application functionality but also its security, performance, and maintainability.

In conclusion, while rooted in technicalities, the world of Docker networking is also a domain of design, strategy, and foresight. Enabling containers on separate networks to communicate is not just about using specific commands or features; it's about understanding the broader application landscape, discerning the nuances of data flow, and crafting a networking strategy that's both efficient and secure. For developers and architects charting the vast seas of container orchestration, understanding the intricacies of inter-network communication isn't just a necessity; it's an art, one that holds the key to unlocking the true potential of modular, scalable, and robust containerized applications.

CHAPTER VIII

Docker Compose

What is Docker Compose?

In the panorama of contemporary software development, the landscape is richly dotted with containers, self-sufficient units that encapsulate application functionality. But while individual containers represent self-contained, atomic units of computation, the real magic unfurls when they join hands, forging orchestrated ensembles that drive multifaceted applications. Introducing Docker Compose, the conductor of this intricate symphony, orchestrating multiple containers' rhythm, pitch, and timbre to create a harmonized performance.

Docker, at its core, revolutionized the paradigm of application deployment by ushering in containerization. These lightweight and efficient containers brought along the promise of consistency: "It works on my machine" became an antiquated adage. But modern applications aren't monolithic; they are often distributed systems comprising numerous components like databases, caches, APIs, and front-end servers. Each can reside in its own container, optimized for its purpose. However, manually running, linking, and managing these myriad containers is an arduous, error-prone endeavor. This is where Docker Compose emerges as the hero, turning the cacophony of individual containers into a synchronized masterpiece.

Docker Compose is a tool designed to define and run multi-container applications. The heart of Docker Compose is its configuration file—docker-compose.yml. This YAML file serves as the sheet music for the application's container symphony, defining each container, its settings, networks, volumes, and the intricate relationships between them. Instead of remembering and executing a barrage of Docker CLI commands, developers simply define their application's structure in this file and then use a single command—docker-compose up—to bring the entire ensemble to life.

The sheer simplicity that Docker Compose brings to the orchestration process masks the profoundness of its capabilities. Within the docker-compose.yml file, not only can services (containers) be defined, but also intricate configurations about their build processes, environment variables, ports, volumes, and networks. Moreover, the relationships between these services—the links, dependencies, and order of startup—are elegantly laid out. This transparency and declarative nature mean that the entire orchestration of an application can be version controlled, shared, and replicated, ensuring that every member of a development team, and every environment where the application runs, echoes the same consistent rhythm.

However, Docker Compose is not just a tool for orchestration but also for development. While production environments might leverage more robust orchestration platforms like Kubernetes or Docker Swarm, Docker Compose shines in local development scenarios. Developers can spawn an environment mirroring production on their local machines, making development and debugging more efficient and reliable. The transient nature of containers means that tearing down and recreating an environment takes seconds, ensuring that testing and iteration cycles are swift and consistent.

A significant advantage of Docker Compose is its scalability. As applications grow, new services might need to be added, or existing ones might need to be scaled horizontally. The declarative nature of the docker-compose.yml file ensures that scaling services, both in terms of configuration and actual runtime instances, is a streamlined process. With a few modifications to the YAML file and simple commands, services can be scaled up or down, allowing developers to simulate and prepare for high-load scenarios.

Yet, while Docker Compose brings with it an array of advantages, it's essential to recognize its scope. It is primarily a development and testing tool, designed for single-host deployments. While it can be used in production, especially for smaller setups, large-scale applications with multi-host requirements might look towards more sophisticated orchestration platforms. However, even in such scenarios, Docker Compose holds value as the starting point—the place where the orchestration journey begins, before graduating to grander platforms.

In conclusion, Docker Compose is the unsung maestro in the Docker ecosystem. While individual containers are the musicians, each skilled in their note, Docker Compose ensures the orchestra plays in harmony, producing a melody greater than the sum of its parts. It encapsulates the complexities of multi-container orchestration behind a veil of simplicity, ensuring developers can focus on what they do best: crafting exceptional software. As the world of containerization continues to evolve, Docker Compose stands as a testament to the importance of orchestration, reminding us that while individual brilliance is noteworthy, true magnificence arises when talents combine in a harmonious concert.

Writing a docker-compose.yml file

In the vast tapestry of containerized applications, Docker stands as an iconic tool, championing the cause of consistent, efficient, and isolated deployments. But while Docker serves as the crucible, molding individual containers, another player in the arena orchestrates these containers into harmonious symphonies: Docker Compose. The heart and soul of Docker Compose is the docker-compose.yml file, a textual representation that provides the blueprint for multi-container applications. Crafting this file is akin to composing music: each note, each chord, and each pause is vital, and when combined in perfect harmony, produces a melody that resonates with clarity and purpose.

The docker-compose.yml file is a YAML (Yet Another Markup Language) formatted document. In its essence, YAML is human-readable and has become a preferred format for configuration files across various tools. The decision to utilize YAML for Docker Compose manifests is consistent with the broader industry trend, prioritizing clarity and simplicity.

The primary section in this file is the services block. Herein lies the declaration of each containerized service that constitutes the application. If one imagines an application comprising a web server, a database, and a caching system, each of these would be a distinct service within this block. The image from which the container is derived is specified for every service. This can be an image pulled from Docker Hub or another registry or built from a local Dockerfile. The build process seamlessly integrates into the orchestration by providing a context and a Dockerfile path, ensuring the image is constructed before the service starts.

Beyond specifying the image or build context, the docker-compose.yml file provides granular control over each service's runtime characteristics. Port mappings ensure the services can communicate with the host or other containers. Environment variables inject configuration parameters into the containers at runtime. Volumes provide persistent storage or facilitate the sharing of data between the host and container, or even among multiple containers.

But the true power of Docker Compose, and by extension the docker-compose.yml file, lies in its ability to define the interplay between services. The relationships between containers are meticulously defined through links, networks, and depends_on directives. A web service can be instructed to wait until the database service is fully operational, ensuring there's no race condition during startup. Through custom networks, containers can communicate with each other, effectively isolating them from external systems, yet allowing them to operate in tandem within this cocooned environment.

Docker Compose also places a heavy emphasis on repeatability and consistency. The volumes and networks sections of the docker-compose.yml file, separate from the services, define these entities at a higher level, ensuring they are consistently applied across all services that utilize them. This abstraction ensures that regardless of the scale or complexity of the application, the underlying infrastructure remains uniform and predictable.

While the mechanics and directives within the docker-compose.yml file are pivotal, there's an artistic angle to its creation as well. Writing this file is not just about understanding Docker or the syntax of YAML. It's about understanding the application, its architecture, and its nuances. It's about visualizing the flow of data, recognizing bottlenecks, and anticipating points of failure. When crafting this file, one doesn't just wear the hat of a developer or a systems engineer. One adopts the role of an architect, designing the intricate maze through which data flows, and the role of a maestro, ensuring each service (or instrument) plays its part in perfect cadence.

Furthermore, the docker-compose.yml file serves another profound purpose in a collaborative setting. It acts as a single source of truth, a reference point that developers, irrespective of their role or expertise, can consult to understand the application's topology. The declarative nature of the file ensures that the entire orchestration can be version-controlled, fostering collaboration, transparency, and traceability.

In conclusion, the docker-compose.yml file, while ostensibly a simple configuration document, is a testament to the intricate ballet of modern, containerized applications. Its lines and blocks capture the essence of the application, its components, and their interrelationships. Crafting this file requires a deep understanding, not just of Docker or YAML, but of the application itself, its needs, its challenges, and its goals. As containerized applications continue to dominate the software landscape, tools like Docker Compose and artifacts like the docker-compose.yml file will remain central, guiding developers and architects in their quest to design, deploy, and manage robust, scalable, and harmonious applications.

Multi-container applications

In the world of software, complexity is a given. As the intricacies of user needs spiral and expand, applications often grow in tandem, evolving from simple scripts to elaborate, multifaceted systems. The age of monolithic applications, where a single codebase was responsible for every facet of functionality, has seen a paradigm shift. Today's software landscape is dominated by multi-container applications, a testament to the architectural principle that champions dividing and conquering complexity.

As the name suggests, multi-container applications are software systems composed of multiple containers. Each container, in its isolated environment, runs a distinct piece of the software puzzle. These containers function symbiotically, each performing its specialized role, yet collectively delivering the seamless experience that a user perceives as a singular application. To the uninitiated, this might seem an unnecessary convolution. Why break an application into multiple parts? The answers lie in the core tenets of software design: modularity, scalability, maintainability, and resilience.

From a design perspective, encapsulating distinct functionalities within separate containers fosters modularity. This separation ensures that each containerized component adheres to the Single Responsibility Principle. A database runs in one container, a caching layer in another, an API server in yet another, and so forth. By ensuring that each container is focused on one task, developers can optimize it for that specific function, enhancing performance and efficiency. Additionally, this modular approach simplifies debugging and maintenance. Should a bug manifest in the API layer, developers can address it without the overhead of wading through the database's or cache's unrelated intricacies.

Scalability is another driving force behind the adoption of multi-container applications. In a monolithic design, scaling requires replicating the entire application, often leading to resource wastage. However, in a multi-container setup, individual components can be scaled independently. If the database is experiencing a bottleneck, only its container can be replicated without needlessly duplicating other application parts. This granularity in scaling ensures resource optimization and cost-effectiveness.

Maintainability, a cornerstone of successful software, also benefits from a multi-container approach. As teams grow and software evolves, having distinct components in separate containers allows for parallel development. Different teams can work on different containers, each focusing on its domain. Deployments, updates, and rollbacks also become more manageable. If a new feature is introduced into the API layer, only that container needs redeployment, leaving the rest of the application untouched and minimizing potential points of failure.

Lastly, resilience, the ability of software to gracefully handle and recover from failures, is enhanced in a multi-container ecosystem. In monolithic systems, a failure in one component could jeopardize the entire application. However, in a multi-container design, the isolated nature of containers means that a failure in one might not necessarily impact the others. Coupled with orchestration tools that can detect and replace failed containers, this design ensures high availability and fault tolerance.

Yet, while the benefits of multi-container applications are compelling, they aren't without challenges. Orchestrating multiple containers, ensuring they communicate seamlessly, maintaining data consistency, and managing inter-container dependencies adds layers of complexity. Tools like Docker Compose, Kubernetes, and Docker Swarm have emerged as solutions to these challenges, offering automated orchestration, scaling, and management features that streamline the complexity of running multi-container systems.

In conclusion, multi-container applications epitomize the ethos of modern software design. They mirror the intricate dance of a ballet performance, where each dancer, akin to a container, performs their distinct role yet contributes to the cohesive narrative of the ballet. In this dance of complexity, while each container moves to its rhythm, the collective choreography, the symphony of interactions, delivers the performance—an application that's modular, scalable, maintainable, and resilient. As software continues to evolve, the embrace of multi-container applications will undoubtedly intensify, underscoring the industry's commitment to building systems that, despite their underlying complexity, deliver seamless, efficient, and reliable user experiences.

CHAPTER IX

Optimizing Docker Images

Using minimal base images

In a world driven by efficiency and performance, minimalism has transcended beyond aesthetics and lifestyle to impact the domain of software design. Within the Docker ecosystem, this ethos is most palpable in the trend of using minimal base images. These lean images have emerged as the lynchpin in the quest for optimized containerization, marrying the principles of efficiency with the necessities of security and performance.

By its very nature, Docker encapsulates applications within containers, ensuring a consistent runtime environment. Each container derives its essence from a base image, which acts as the foundational layer, containing the essential software, libraries, and binaries necessary for the application to run. The choice of this base image is crucial, influencing not just the size of the container but also its boot time, vulnerability profile, and maintenance overhead.

Historically, containers often leveraged substantial, general-purpose base images. These images, often derivatives of full-fledged operating systems like Ubuntu or CentOS, brought with them a plethora of utilities and libraries. While such a broad assortment might seem advantageous, it introduced unnecessary bloat. Most applications utilized only a fraction of the utilities bundled within, meaning that a significant portion of the container's footprint was redundant. This redundancy wasn't merely an issue of wasted space; it translated to longer image pull times, increased storage costs, and prolonged container boot times.

Introducing minimal base images—lean, stripped-down images tailored to provide only what's essential for running applications. The philosophy behind these images is simple: "If you don't need it, don't include it." Images like Alpine Linux have gained immense popularity in this context. With sizes measuring in mere megabytes, compared to the gigabytes of more extensive counterparts, Alpine and similar minimal images offer a compact solution without compromising on essential functionalities.

However, the allure of minimal base images isn't confined to their reduced size. A critical, often underscored benefit lies in the realm of security. Every piece of software, be it a library, utility, or binary, carries with it the potential for vulnerabilities. A larger image, laden with unnecessary components, increases the attack surface, providing more potential points of exploitation. By virtue of their trimmed content, minimal images inherently possess fewer potential vulnerabilities. When one couples this with the fact that smaller images also mean faster security scans, it's evident that minimal base images bolster proactive and reactive security measures.

Maintainability is another facet enhanced by minimalism. With fewer components within the image, the overhead of updates, patches, and compatibility checks is significantly reduced. This streamlined maintenance process saves time and ensures that containers remain in their optimal state, minimizing technical debt and potential system drift.

However, like all solutions, minimal base images aren't without challenges. Their lean nature means developers might occasionally find some utilities or libraries missing, requiring manual inclusion. This need for manual intervention could introduce a learning curve, especially for those accustomed to fuller images. Yet, in many scenarios, the benefits of lean images—speed, security, and simplicity—outweigh the initial adjustment period.

It's also worth noting that while minimal base images offer many advantages, they aren't a one-size-fits-all solution. Specific applications or environments might necessitate more comprehensive base images. The key lies in discernment, evaluating the application's requirements, and weighing the trade-offs.

In conclusion, the shift towards minimal base images in Docker is emblematic of the broader trend in software—optimizing for what's necessary and shedding the excess. In a landscape where efficiency, security, and performance are paramount, these lean images stand as a testament to the belief that less can be more. As containerization continues to dominate the deployment paradigm, the role of minimal base images will undoubtedly grow, guiding developers and organizations toward more streamlined, secure, and efficient application delivery.

Multi-stage builds

In the vast universe of Docker, where efficiency and optimization hold sway, multi-stage builds have emerged as an instrumental tool, allowing developers to craft lean, robust, and efficient images. They represent Docker's acknowledgment of the diverse needs of the container lifecycle, bridging the gap between development dependencies and runtime necessities.

To appreciate the importance of multi-stage builds, it's vital to understand the journey of containerized applications. During development, applications often require a host of tools and dependencies. Compilers, build tools, test frameworks, and debugging utilities, among others, play a pivotal role in shaping the software. However, many of these tools become redundant once the software is ready for deployment. A runtime environment typically needs only the compiled application and its direct runtime dependencies. This dichotomy presents a challenge: How does one build an image supporting development and production without carrying unnecessary baggage?

Introducing multi-stage builds, Docker's elegant answer to this problem. Multi-stage builds allow a Dockerfile to define multiple intermediate images, each tailored for specific application lifecycle stages. These intermediate images can have their own base images and sets of instructions. The beauty lies in the final stage, where artifacts from previous stages can be copied over, while leaving behind everything that's non-essential. The result? A lean, optimized image tailored for deployment, devoid of any development-related overhead.

The benefits of this approach are manifold. Firstly, there's a stark reduction in the final image size. Multi-stage builds produce lightweight images by excluding superfluous tools and libraries that were essential during the build phase but redundant for runtime. This translates to faster pull times, reduced storage costs, and quicker container start times—factors directly impacting deployment agility and scalability.

Security is another domain that stands to gain from multi-stage builds. Every component in an image, from binaries to libraries, represents a potential vulnerability vector. Multi-stage builds inherently reduce the attack surface by minimizing the components in the final image. This translates to a more secure runtime environment and ensures quicker security scans, further bolstering the image's security posture.

Yet, multi-stage builds' merits aren't confined to size and security. They also introduce clarity and organization into the Dockerfile. Developers can logically separate build-time instructions from runtime configurations, offering a clearer picture of the container's lifecycle. This enhanced readability ensures that Dockerfiles are not just scripts but well-documented representations of the containerization process.

However, like all tools, multi-stage builds come with their own set of considerations. Developers must be judicious in determining what to carry forward to the final image. This requires a clear understanding of the application's runtime dependencies to ensure that no crucial component is inadvertently left behind. Additionally, while multi-stage builds introduce clarity into Dockerfiles, they also add length and complexity. Proper commenting and documentation become paramount to ensure that the Dockerfile remains comprehensible.

Despite these considerations, the advantages of multi-stage builds are compelling, especially for production-ready containers. They encapsulate Docker's ethos of efficiency, marrying the comprehensive needs of development with the minimalist requirements of deployment.

In conclusion, multi-stage builds represent one of Docker's many endeavors to streamline containerization. They acknowledge the evolving needs of applications, from inception to deployment, ensuring that each stage is catered to without compromising the next. In a world driven by performance, agility, and security, multi-stage builds stand out as a beacon of optimization, urging developers to craft images as efficient as they are effective. As Docker continues to cement its place in the software deployment landscape, tools and features like multi-stage builds will play a pivotal role in defining the contours of optimized, effective, and elegant containerization.

Reducing image sizes

In the realm of containerized deployment, where Docker has emerged as a paragon of efficiency, the size of Docker images carries profound significance. Large images consume more storage and elongate deployment cycles, slow down scaling operations, and pose security concerns. Hence, reducing image sizes is not merely a pursuit of optimization but a necessary strategy to ensure agile, secure, and efficient application delivery.

At the heart of Docker's modus operandi is encapsulating applications and their dependencies within containers to ensure consistent execution environments. Each Docker image forms the blueprint of a container, containing the software, libraries, and configurations required for the application. However, the intrinsic value of an image is not just in what it has but also in what it omits. As applications grow and evolve, Docker images can inadvertently accrue unnecessary files, outdated libraries, and redundant layers, leading to image bloat. Addressing this bloat is crucial, and several strategies can be employed to achieve leaner images.

The first and most fundamental step in reducing image size is the informed choice of the base image. While it might be tempting to opt for comprehensive images that offer a wide array of utilities, such images often introduce superfluous components. For many applications, a minimal base image, like Alpine Linux, offers a compact foundation without compromising essential functionalities. Alpine, for instance, starts at a mere 5MB, providing a lightweight alternative to heftier images based on more significant distributions.

By embracing such minimal base images, developers can begin their containerization journey on a note of compactness.

Yet, the choice of the base image is just the starting point. How applications and dependencies are added to the image plays a crucial role in determining its final size. Here, multi-stage builds offer a potent tool. As discussed previously, multi-stage builds allow developers to create intermediate images tailored for specific phases of the application lifecycle. Only the necessary artifacts are retained by the final stage, ensuring that development tools, build caches, and intermediary files don't bloat the image.

Another impactful strategy is the careful management and optimization of Docker layers. Each instruction in a Dockerfile creates a new layer, and while layers offer caching benefits, they can also add to the image size. Combining commands, cleaning up in the same layer where files are created or temporary data is written, and being mindful of the order of instructions can help crafting optimized layers. Moreover, removing temporary files, caches, and unneeded packages within the same instruction that creates them ensures that the bloat doesn't get written to the final image.

It's also worthwhile to periodically review and update images. Over time, outdated libraries, deprecated tools, and accumulated logs can inflate image sizes. Regularly revisiting Dockerfiles, updating the base image, and pruning unnecessary components ensure that images remain lean and up-to-date. Additionally, tools like Dive or the docker image history command can provide insights into each layer of an image, helping developers identify and eliminate redundancies.

Beyond these manual optimizations, developers can leverage tools and utilities specifically designed to trim Docker images. Solutions like DockerSlim can analyze and minimize images without changing the Dockerfiles. Such tools reduce image sizes and enhance security by removing potential vulnerability vectors.

In conclusion, the endeavor to reduce Docker image sizes embodies the broader ethos of modern software deployment—achieving more with less. As the digital landscape becomes increasingly dynamic, the agility, speed, and security offered by compact Docker images become invaluable. By making informed choices, leveraging multi-stage builds, optimizing layers, and utilizing specialized tools, developers can craft images that are not just smaller but also more efficient and secure. In the intricate dance of containerization, where every byte and layer counts, reducing image sizes is both an art and a necessity, underpinning the promise of seamless, efficient, and scalable application delivery.

CHAPTER X

Security Best Practices

Running containers securely

Docker containers stand out as pockets of efficiency, streamlining development and deployment processes in the intricate weave of modern software ecosystems. However, as with any technological marvel, they come with their own set of challenges, notably in the realm of security. While Docker containers encapsulate applications in isolated environments, ensuring their secure execution requires deliberate strategies and practices. This section delves deep into the nuances of running Docker containers securely, exploring the intersection of containerization and cybersecurity.

The intrinsic strength of Docker containers lies in their isolated nature. By leveraging features of the Linux kernel, such as namespaces and cgroups, Docker ensures that each container runs in its own environment, shielded from others. This isolation serves as the first line of defense against malicious activities. However, while isolation offers protection, it's only as robust as its configuration. Ensuring that containers run with the least privilege principle is paramount. This means that containers should only be granted permissions essential for their operation and nothing more. For instance, running containers as non-root users minimizes potential damage should the container be compromised.

Further bolstering this shield of isolation is the proper management of Docker images. The source and integrity of these images play a pivotal role in container security. Obtaining images from trusted repositories and verified vendors is of utmost importance. Scanning official base images for vulnerabilities and regularly updating them ensures that containers aren't built on compromised foundations. Tools like Clair or Trivy can assist developers in scanning images for known security issues, ensuring that containers start their lifecycle on a security note.

But even with a secure foundation, the dynamic nature of containers necessitates real-time safeguards. Implementing runtime security monitoring can detect and respond to anomalies in container behavior. By establishing a baseline of normal container operations, deviations from this norm—be it a sudden spike in resource usage, unauthorized network calls, or unexpected file modifications—can be flagged and addressed. Solutions like Falco, a cloud-native runtime security project, can assist in this endeavor, offering real-time alerting on anomalous container activities.

Network configurations, too, play a pivotal role in container security. Since many applications involve inter-container communications or access to external networks, ensuring secure networking is non-negotiable. Employing network segmentation, where containers are grouped based on functionalities and are only allowed to communicate with necessary components, limits the potential blast radius of a security incident. Implementing firewalls, employing secure protocols, and disabling inter-container communication, unless necessary further enhance the network security posture.

Docker, aware of the security imperatives, has endowed users with built-in tools to enhance container security. Seccomp (secure computing mode), for instance, allows administrators to define system call filters, restricting containers from making potentially dangerous system calls. Similarly, AppArmor and SELinux offer mandatory access control frameworks that can be tailored to container requirements. Leveraging these built-in functionalities ensures containers operate within a well-defined security perimeter, shielded from potential exploits.

While internal configurations and tools bolster container security, external solutions, especially those tailored for container environments, enhance multifold protection. Container security platforms, like Aqua Trivy or Sysdig Secure, offer comprehensive security solutions, from image scanning to runtime monitoring. Implementing such platforms provides an additional layer of protection, often complemented by insights and analytics to continually refine the security strategy.

Of course, in the realm of security, human factors play as significant a role as technological measures. Ensuring that the development and operations teams are well-versed in best security practices is essential. This includes understanding the nuances of Docker security, being aware of the latest vulnerabilities and patches, and implementing a robust incident response protocol. Regular training sessions, workshops, and drills can instill a culture of security, ensuring that the human elements of the container lifecycle are as fortified as the technological aspects.

Lastly, it's essential to acknowledge that no solution is foolproof in the ever-evolving landscape of cybersecurity. Continuous monitoring, regular audits, and a proactive approach to security are the cornerstones of a robust container security posture. By keeping abreast of the latest threats, vulnerabilities, and patches and continually refining security strategies based on insights and experiences, organizations can ensure that their Docker containers run securely, efficiently, and effectively.

In conclusion, while Docker containers offer many advantages in software deployment, ensuring their secure execution requires a confluence of strategies, tools, and practices. From the foundational security of images to real-time runtime monitoring, leveraging built-in Docker security tools to implementing external security platforms, and securing network configurations to human-centric security training, each facet plays a pivotal role in safeguarding containers. In the delicate ballet of containerized applications, where agility, efficiency, and security intertwine, running Docker containers securely stands out as both an imperative and an art, anchoring the promise of containerization in the bedrock of cybersecurity.

Scanning images for vulnerabilities

In the golden age of containerization, Docker has revolutionized how we think about, develop, and deploy software. But as with any transformative technology, there's a caveat: the ever-present specter of security vulnerabilities. As software environments grow more complex, developers often utilize pre-existing Docker images as the foundation for their applications. But are these foundations secure? This question underscores the critical importance of scanning Docker images for vulnerabilities. By delving into the why, how, and what of this crucial process, this section aims to shed light on the pivotal role image scanning plays in safeguarding containerized applications.

Let's begin by understanding the importance of scanning. Docker images act as blueprints from which containers spring to life. Like architectural blueprints, if there's a flaw in the design, the final structure—the running container in this case—will inherit that flaw. These vulnerabilities, whether in the base operating system, libraries, or the application itself, can be exploited by malicious actors, leading to breaches, data leaks, or even total system compromise. Developers can preemptively counteract potential security threats by identifying and rectifying these vulnerabilities at the image level.

The Docker ecosystem is vast and ever-changing. Images get updated, libraries evolve, and new vulnerabilities emerge almost daily. A Docker image deemed secure a month ago might today be riddled with exploitable vulnerabilities due to changes in its constituent components. This dynamic nature underscores the necessity of regular, if not continuous, vulnerability scanning. Moreover, with the shift-left paradigm in DevOps, where security is embedded early in the development lifecycle, integrating image scanning during the CI/CD pipeline can ensure that insecure images never make it to production.

The mechanics of vulnerability scanning can be likened to a meticulous detective combing through every element of a Docker image. Scanning tools maintain extensive databases of known vulnerabilities, sourced from repositories like the Common Vulnerabilities and Exposures (CVE) system. When an image is scanned, every layer—each file, library, and dependency—is cross-referenced with this database. If there's a match, the tool flags it, often providing details about the vulnerability, its severity, and potential remediations.

Several open-source and proprietary tools have emerged in response to the need for robust Docker image scanning. Open-source solutions like Clair, developed by CoreOS, or Trivy by Aqua Security, provide comprehensive scanning capabilities. They are frequently updated, ensuring they can detect the latest vulnerabilities. On the proprietary front, solutions like Aqua Trivy, Snyk, and Anchore offer additional features, from integration capabilities with CI/CD tools to advanced reporting and analytics. The choice between these tools often hinges on specific organizational requirements, budgets, and preferred workflows.

However, simply identifying vulnerabilities is only half the battle. The subsequent—and arguably more crucial—step is remediation. Once a vulnerability is detected, developers must address it. This could involve updating a library to its latest secure version, switching to a different base image, or refactoring application code parts. Some scanning tools go a step further by identifying vulnerabilities and suggesting fixes, making the remediation process more streamlined.

An often overlooked facet of vulnerability scanning is its ability to educate and inform. For development teams, the feedback from scanning tools can be a revelation, highlighting potential security pitfalls they might have been unaware of. Over time, this feedback can foster a more security-conscious development culture. Developers begin to recognize patterns, make more informed choices about libraries and base images, and even proactively seek out secure coding practices. Vulnerability scanning can act as a continuous security training tool ingrained within the development workflow.

Yet, as pivotal as image scanning is, it's essential to recognize its limitations. While scanning tools are adept at identifying known vulnerabilities, they might not detect zero-day vulnerabilities— newly discovered vulnerabilities that are not yet in the public domain—or vulnerabilities that arise due to specific configuration settings. Furthermore, vulnerability scanning focuses predominantly on the image's contents, not its runtime behavior. As such, it should be complemented by runtime security monitoring and other security best practices.

In conclusion, scanning Docker images for vulnerabilities is a sentinel in the container security landscape. It guards against known vulnerabilities and plays an instrumental role in fostering a security-first development ethos. The intricate dance of developing in a containerized world, with its myriad images, libraries, and dependencies, is fraught with potential security pitfalls. Through diligent, regular vulnerability scanning, developers and organizations can confidently navigate this dance, ensuring their applications are efficient and agile and secure. As containerization continues its march as a dominant force in software deployment, the spotlight on vulnerability scanning will only grow brighter, heralding its indispensable role in safeguarding the future of software development.

Keeping Docker updated

The rapid growth and widespread adoption of containerization have made Docker synonymous with modern software development and deployment. Docker allows developers to design, test, and ship their applications in isolated environments called containers. These containers can be seamlessly transferred across diverse infrastructures, from a developer's local workstation to vast cloud architectures, ensuring consistent behavior. However, as with any software solution, the dynamism of the technology landscape means Docker is frequently updated to address vulnerabilities, enhance performance, and introduce new features. This section delves deep into the importance of keeping Docker updated and the potential ramifications of neglecting this crucial practice.

To appreciate the significance of regular updates, one must first understand the layered structure of Docker. A Docker environment comprises the Docker engine itself, the images used to instantiate containers, and the containers that run based on these images. Each of these components, if outdated, can be a potential weak link, rendering the entire environment susceptible to inefficiencies or even breaches. Hence, the argument for keeping Docker updated is as much about fortifying security as it is about harnessing improved functionality and performance.

Security stands as the paramount reason for regular updates. In our interconnected digital age, software vulnerabilities are constantly being discovered. While some of these vulnerabilities may be benign, malicious actors can exploit others to compromise systems. Given Docker's centrality in many organizational infrastructures, a security flaw in Docker can have cascading effects, jeopardizing the integrity of numerous applications. Updates often include patches for these known vulnerabilities, ensuring systems are not exposed. Neglecting these updates is akin to leaving the doors of one's digital fortress ajar, inviting unwarranted intrusions.

Beyond immediate security concerns, updates frequently bring performance enhancements. The Docker development community, driven by feedback from millions of users, is continually refining the software to make it faster, more resource-efficient, and more compatible with diverse system configurations. By not updating Docker, organizations may inadvertently handcuff themselves to suboptimal performance. Over time, these inefficiencies can accumulate, leading to increased operational costs, slower application response times, and diminished user satisfaction.

Furthermore, Docker updates often introduce new features or improve existing ones. These enhancements range from better orchestration tools, improved logging and monitoring functionalities, and more intuitive APIs. By proactively updating Docker, developers and operations teams can leverage these state-of-the-art features, ensuring that their workflows are efficient and aligned with industry best practices. The alternative, sticking with older versions, might mean forgoing powerful tools that can simplify development, testing, and deployment processes.

The importance of updates extends to Docker images as well. These images, which serve as container templates, are often based on other foundational images. For instance, an image running a Python application might be built on a base image of a specific Linux distribution. The application-specific and foundational layers can have vulnerabilities or outdated components. Therefore, it's essential to keep these images updated alongside updating Docker itself. The Docker community and image maintainers usually release updated images in response to known vulnerabilities or to include newer software versions. Regularly pulling these updated images ensures that containers instantiated from them are secure and optimized.

Now, while the arguments for regular updates are compelling, updating Docker must be approached judiciously. Blindly updating Docker in a production environment without adequate testing can lead to unforeseen complications. For instance, newer versions might have changes that render them incompatible with specific legacy systems or configurations. Hence, a best practice is to have a staged approach. Updates should first be tested in isolated, non-critical environments. Once their stability and compatibility are ascertained, they can be rolled out to more critical environments. Automated testing tools and continuous integration pipelines can assist in this phased rollout, ensuring that updates don't disrupt existing workflows.

In addition to a staged approach, it's beneficial to maintain an awareness of Docker's release cycles and update channels. Docker usually has multiple release channels, such as stable and edge. While the stable channel is designed for reliability, the edge channel includes the latest features and updates. Depending on an organization's appetite for risk and its need for cutting-edge features, it can choose the appropriate channel for updates. However, regardless of the selected channel, vigilance is critical. Keeping an eye on Docker's official release notes, subscribing to update notifications, or even participating in relevant community forums can ensure that teams are not caught off-guard by crucial updates.

In conclusion, Docker requires meticulous maintenance as an instrumental force in modern software paradigms. Regular updates are not just a chore but a commitment to security, performance, and technological prowess. By embracing updates, organizations can fortify their digital infrastructures, optimize their workflows, and position themselves at the forefront of technological innovation. Conversely, neglecting updates can have dire consequences, from breaches and system downtimes to eroded competitive advantages. Thus, in the dynamic dance of software development and deployment, keeping Docker updated is not just a step but a leap towards a more secure, efficient, and innovative future.

CHAPTER XI

Continuous Integration and Deployment with Docker

Integrating Docker with CI/CD pipelines

In the fast-paced world of software development, two trends have surged to prominence in recent years: Docker and Continuous Integration/Continuous Deployment (CI/CD) pipelines. On the surface, these might seem like independent evolutions. Docker, a platform that facilitates containerization, allows for application consistency across varying development and production environments. CI/CD, on the other hand, is an ethos and methodology that emphasizes the frequent, automated integration and deployment of code. Yet, when combined, Docker and CI/CD merge to form a potent partnership, revolutionizing how developers build, test, and deploy applications. This section explores the deep synergy between Docker and CI/CD pipelines and sheds light on the transformative potential of their integration.

To appreciate the power of integrating Docker with CI/CD, it's vital to understand the challenges that developers traditionally face. Moving code from a developer's local machine to a production server was historically fraught with inconsistencies. Phrases like "it worked on my machine" symbolized the discrepancies between development, staging, and production environments. These inconsistencies, arising from differences in configurations, libraries, or even operating systems, often led to unexpected bugs, costly rollbacks, and wasted developer hours.

Introducing Docker. Docker's core proposition, containerization, seeks to encapsulate applications and their dependencies into isolated units, known as containers. These containers are both lightweight and consistent, ensuring that an application behaves uniformly, regardless of where the container runs. This paradigm-shifting capability immediately addressed the age-old "it worked on my machine" problem, ensuring that if an application runs smoothly in a Docker container on a developer's local machine, it will do so in any other environment that supports Docker.

Now, combining Docker's capabilities with the aspirations of CI/CD. At its heart, CI/CD is about speeding up the software lifecycle, ensuring that code changes are continuously integrated, tested, and deployed to production. The methodology fosters rapid feedback loops, early bug detection, and swift feature releases. However, for CI/CD to function optimally requires an environment where code can be seamlessly and predictably moved across various stages, from integration testing to staging to production. It's here that Docker's promise of consistency becomes invaluable.

By integrating Docker with CI/CD pipelines, developers can ensure that every code change, once committed, is tested in a Dockerized environment that mirrors production. If the tests pass and the code integrates smoothly, it can be automatically deployed—again, within Docker containers—to staging or production servers. This integration eradicates environment-specific anomalies and ensures unforeseen discrepancies do not hamper the CI/CD pipeline's rapid, automated workflows.

Moreover, Docker's inherent portability facilitates the creation of transient testing environments. In a CI/CD setup, every code commit can spawn a temporary, Dockerized environment where integration tests run. Post-testing, this environment can be swiftly torn down, conserving resources. Such ephemeral environments, made feasible by Docker's lightweight nature, allow for parallel testing of multiple code commits, further accelerating the CI/CD pipeline.

Another profound advantage of integrating Docker with CI/CD is the modularization of applications through microservices. Modern applications are increasingly being architected as collections of loosely coupled, independently deployable services. By its very design, Docker is conducive to such microservices, allowing each service to reside in its own container. When combined with CI/CD, this microservices architecture allows for the independent testing and deployment of individual services. If a team changes a specific service, only that service must move through the CI/CD pipeline, ensuring rapid, targeted deployments without affecting the broader application ecosystem.

Yet, while the benefits of integrating Docker with CI/CD are diverse, the process has its intricacies. Developers must craft precise

Dockerfiles that dictate how Docker containers are built. CI/CD tools must be configured to orchestrate Docker operations, from building images to running containers. Additionally, considerations around Docker image storage, networking between containers, and managing stateful data within containers must be addressed to ensure a seamless CI/CD flow. Tools like Docker Compose, which allows for the definition and management of multi-container Docker applications, can aid in simplifying some of these complexities.

In conclusion, Docker and CI/CD, though conceived as solutions to distinct challenges in the software lifecycle, converge to offer an integrated, robust platform for modern development. Docker's promise of consistency and portability dovetails perfectly with CI/CD's ambition for rapid, automated code flows. Together, they eliminate the traditional pain points of development and catalyze innovations like microservices. For organizations striving for agility, efficiency, and reliability in their development processes, integrating Docker with CI/CD isn't just an option—it's an imperative. By harnessing this synergy, developers can enhance their workflows and elevate the very paradigms of software creation and delivery.

Automated testing with Docker

In the lexicon of software development, the phrase "automated testing" evokes sentiments of reliability, efficiency, and repeatability. These qualities are paramount in the era of rapid software iterations, where consistent code quality and prompt feedback loops are not mere conveniences, but necessities. Yet, as crucial as automated testing is, it's often plagued by environmental discrepancies that can render test results unpredictable. This unpredictability can, in turn, negate the very advantages automated testing promises. Docker—a platform championing containerization—and its transformative effect on the automated testing landscape. By integrating Docker's capabilities with automated testing frameworks, developers can cultivate a robust and reliable testing ecosystem, further refining the software development process.

To understand the profound impact Docker can have on automated testing, one must first appreciate the pain points that pervade traditional testing approaches. A dedicated test environment—often physically separate or virtually partitioned—is used to run automated tests in a conventional testing setup. While this environment is supposed to mirror production, discrepancies often arise. These discrepancies, stemming from differences in configurations, dependencies, or even underlying hardware, can cause tests to pass in the testing environment but fail in production, leading to the notorious "it worked in testing" conundrum.

Docker offers an elegant solution to this predicament through its core principle: containerization. Docker essentially allows developers to encapsulate applications—and their entire runtime environment—into isolated containers. These containers guarantee consistency regardless of where they are executed, be it a developer's local machine, a testing server, or a production cluster. This means that a test running inside a Docker container will identically interact with its environment, irrespective of the underlying infrastructure. Such determinism is invaluable in automated testing, ensuring that tests genuinely validate code against production-like conditions.

Beyond consistency, Docker offers several other advantages that elevate the automated testing process. Firstly, Docker's containers are ephemeral. Post-testing, they can be effortlessly discarded and replaced by fresh instances for subsequent test runs. This transient nature ensures that tests always commence clean and predictable, eliminating the risk of lingering data or configurations influencing test outcomes. Moreover, Docker's lightweight architecture facilitates parallelism. Multiple test suites can run concurrently in separate containers, dramatically reducing the time taken for comprehensive test coverage.

Integrating Docker into automated testing also simplifies dependency management. Traditional testing often necessitates a complex setup process, involving the installation of specific software versions, databases, and other dependencies. With Docker, all these prerequisites can be codified into a Dockerfile—a script instructing Docker on building a container. Once this Dockerfile is authored, spawning a fully configured testing environment becomes as simple as executing a single Docker command. This ease of setup streamlines the testing process and ensures that every test run starts with the exact intended configurations.

Furthermore, Docker's compatibility with many Continuous Integration (CI) tools, such as Jenkins, Travis CI, and CircleCI, amplifies its utility in automated testing. CI tools can be configured to trigger Docker-based test runs automatically whenever code is committed, ensuring that potential issues are identified at the earliest stages of the development cycle. By weaving Docker into the CI tapestry, developers can cultivate a fully automated, consistent, and rapid feedback mechanism, reinforcing the principles of agile and DevOps methodologies.

However, as transformative as Docker's impact on automated testing can be, there are nuances and best practices developers should be mindful of. For instance, by default, Docker containers come with a minimalistic set of tools and libraries. Developers must ensure that their Docker images—the blueprints for containers—are judiciously crafted to include all necessary testing tools and dependencies. Additionally, networking between Docker containers, especially in scenarios where tests span multiple services or databases, needs careful configuration to ensure seamless communication. Lastly, while Docker guarantees environmental consistency, the onus remains on developers to write comprehensive, well-architected tests that adequately validate software functionalities.

In conclusion, Docker's fusion with automated testing represents a paradigm shift in software validation. By assuaging the age-old challenges of environmental discrepancies, complex setups, and lack of determinism, Docker empowers developers to harness the full potential of automated testing. The benefits of this integration—rapid feedback, consistent results, and streamlined processes—are manifold, leading to enhanced code quality, reduced debugging overhead, and accelerated release cycles. As software development evolves, driven by user demands and technological advancements, tools and methodologies that enhance reliability and efficiency will always be in vogue. In the confluence of Docker and automated testing, developers have a potent ally, poised to shape the future of software craftsmanship.

Deployment strategies

The advent of containerization, with Docker at its forefront, has reshaped the landscape of software deployment. Gone are the days when system administrators painstakingly provisioned servers, wary of intricate dependencies and environmental disparities. Instead, Docker's promise of "build once, run anywhere" offers a panacea for these age-old deployment woes. But beyond this core tenet, Docker empowers developers and operations teams with flexible deployment strategies, ensuring software is delivered efficiently, reliably, and with minimal disruption. This section delves into the transformative deployment strategies facilitated by Docker and their implications on the modern software delivery process.

Historically, software deployment has been fraught with challenges. The deployment phase was often unpredictable even if development and testing cycles proceeded without a hitch. Minor differences between staging and production environments, be it a library version or an OS patch, could culminate in catastrophic failures. Docker's containerization model, which encapsulates an application and its dependencies into a consistent environment, dramatically mitigates these risks. However, the true potential of Docker in deployment strategies emerges when one considers the granularity, speed, and automation it introduces into the deployment pipeline.

One of the seminal strategies facilitated by Docker is the blue-green deployment. In this approach, two parallel environments exist: the 'blue' environment, which currently serves live traffic, and the 'green' environment, which is the new version to be deployed. Once the 'green' version is thoroughly tested and ready, traffic is seamlessly switched from 'blue' to 'green.' The beauty of this approach lies in its risk mitigation. If issues arise post-deployment, traffic can instantly revert to the 'blue' environment, ensuring uninterrupted service. Docker's ability to quickly spin up identical containers makes creating and managing these parallel environments both efficient and consistent.

Another deployment strategy redefined by Docker is the canary release. Named after the proverbial "canary in a coal mine," this strategy involves deploying a new software version to a small subset of users. If this "canary" deployment proves successful, it's gradually rolled out to the broader user base. Docker's container orchestration tools, like Docker Swarm or Kubernetes, allow for precise control over traffic routing and load balancing, making the incremental release of canaries manageable and measurable.

For applications demanding high availability, rolling updates present an attractive deployment strategy. In this approach, the new version is incrementally deployed across the infrastructure, one server or container at a time, until the entire fleet is updated. This phased rollout ensures no downtime, as a portion of the infrastructure is always available to serve user requests. Docker's orchestration capabilities shine here, allowing for automated rolling updates with built-in health checks. If a newly deployed container exhibits anomalies, the rollout can be paused or rolled back, ensuring system stability.

Beyond these strategies, Docker's inherent modularity and scalability empower even more nuanced deployment tactics, such as feature toggles. Instead of deploying entire new versions, specific features within an application can be toggled on or off. While feature toggles aren't exclusive to Docker, the platform's ability to maintain consistent environments ensures that toggled features behave predictably across diverse infrastructures.

However, successful deployment strategies with Docker aren't solely predicated on the platform's capabilities. Best practices and due diligence play a crucial role. For instance, monitoring and logging are indispensable. When deploying new versions, especially in incremental strategies like canary releases or rolling updates, monitoring tools must be in place to promptly detect and address anomalies. Similarly, logging ensures that any post-deployment issues can be swiftly diagnosed and rectified.

Additionally, while Docker offers a consistent environment, it's imperative to maintain parity across all stages of the software lifecycle. The adage, "as close to production as possible," should be the guiding principle. This ensures that when a new version is deployed, be it via blue-green, canary, or rolling updates, it behaves as expected because it's been developed and tested in an environment mirroring production.

In conclusion, Docker's rise has not just revolutionized application containerization but has also redefined deployment strategies. Its promise of consistency, coupled with the granularity and control it offers, allows for deployment tactics that are both flexible and reliable. From the instantaneous switchovers of blue-green deployments to the measured, phased approaches of canary releases and rolling updates, Docker ensures software delivery is efficient, scalable, and resilient. Yet, as with all powerful tools, the onus remains on developers and operations teams to use Docker judiciously, adhering to best practices and continuously monitoring deployments. In doing so, they can harness Docker's full potential, ensuring software reaches its audience seamlessly and delivers the unwavering reliability that today's digital age demands.

CHAPTER XII

Docker in the Cloud

Using Docker with cloud providers (AWS, GCP, Azure)

In today's world of ubiquitous cloud computing, Docker has emerged as a force multiplier, seamlessly bridging the gap between local development environments and expansive cloud infrastructures. Major cloud service providers like the Amazon Web Services (or AWS), Google Cloud Platform (or GCP), and Microsoft Azure have recognized Docker's transformative potential, integrating it into their ecosystems to offer myriad services. This synergy between Docker and cloud platforms has simplified deployment and scaling of applications and introduced a new era of agility and efficiency in cloud computing. This section seeks to elucidate the confluence of Docker with these three cloud giants and the ensuing advantages for developers and businesses.

To begin, consider Amazon Web Services (AWS), a behemoth in the cloud industry. AWS's integration with Docker is manifested in its Amazon Elastic Container Service (ECS) service. ECS allows developers to run Docker containers at scale effortlessly. With just a few configurations, a developer can deploy a Dockerized application onto a cluster of virtual machines without the intricacies of managing the underlying infrastructure. Amazon ECS even dovetails with AWS Fargate, a serverless compute engine for containers, allowing developers to deploy Docker containers without provisioning servers, enhancing simplicity and cost-efficiency. Moreover, for those more inclined towards Kubernetes, AWS offers the Elastic Kubernetes Service (EKS), ensuring Docker containers can be orchestrated using the popular Kubernetes system seamlessly within the AWS environment.

Meanwhile, the Google Cloud Platform (GCP) has not been a mere spectator in this Docker-cloud amalgamation. Google Kubernetes Engine (GKE) represents GCP's commitment to facilitating Docker deployments. Kubernetes, originally designed by Google, finds a natural home in GCP. GKE allows for effortless orchestration of Docker containers, handling tasks like cluster management and auto-scaling, thus ensuring applications are both resilient and performant. GCP also provides a Container Registry, a private storage solution for Docker images, ensuring they are securely stored and can be efficiently accessed when deploying containers. Additionally, Google Cloud Run offers a fully managed compute platform that automatically scales stateless Docker containers, reflecting GCP's versatility in catering to Kubernetes enthusiasts and those seeking more straightforward solutions.

Microsoft Azure, not to be outdone, has made significant strides in integrating Docker into its fold. Azure Kubernetes Service (AKS) offers a managed Kubernetes environment, making it straightforward to deploy, manage, and scale Dockerized applications using Kubernetes on Azure. Azure also offers the Azure Container

Instances (ACI) service, which is geared toward those looking for a lightweight solution to run their Docker containers without the complexities of orchestration. One of the standout features of Azure's integration with Docker is the ACI-Docker integration. This allows developers to use the Docker CLI, a tool they're familiar with, to run containers directly in Azure, thereby merging the simplicity of Docker commands with the power of Azure's infrastructure.

Integrating Docker with these cloud providers isn't just a matter of convenience; it heralds numerous benefits. Firstly, portability is enhanced. Docker's promise of "build once, run anywhere" finds a broader playground in the cloud. Developers can build and test their Docker containers locally and deploy them to any cloud provider without modifications. This mitigates the age-old dilemma of "it works on my machine," ensuring consistency across development, staging, and production environments.

Scalability is another significant advantage. Docker's lightweight nature, combined with the expansive infrastructure of cloud providers, ensures applications can scale out to handle increased load seamlessly. Whether the auto-scaling capabilities of Kubernetes services like EKS, GKE, and AKS, or the simplicity of serverless solutions like Fargate and Cloud Run, applications can dynamically adapt to varying loads without manual intervention.

Furthermore, this Docker-cloud synergy enhances cost efficiency. Docker's efficient utilization of system resources, combined with the pay-as-you-go model of cloud providers, ensures businesses only pay for the resources they consume. Serverless solutions like Fargate and

Cloud Run further this cost optimization, as there's no need to provision or manage servers.

In conclusion, integrating Docker with significant cloud providers AWS, GCP, and Azure has set the stage for a new paradigm in cloud computing. This symbiotic relationship combines Docker's consistency and efficiency with the scalability and breadth of services offered by cloud giants. Developers and businesses are the ultimate beneficiaries, reaping the rewards of seamless deployments, enhanced scalability, and cost optimization. As cloud computing continues to evolve, the alliance of Docker with these cloud platforms promises even more innovative solutions, ensuring the needs of modern applications are met with agility, resilience, and efficiency.

Kubernetes basics and its relation to Docker

In the ever-evolving domain of software development and deployment, two technologies have become game-changers: Docker and Kubernetes. Both have redefined how applications are developed, deployed, and scaled, presenting novel solutions to age-old challenges. At first glance, they may appear to serve similar purposes, but their functionalities and their synergy carve out a unique niche in the modern IT infrastructure. Through this section, we delve into the foundational aspects of Kubernetes, its relationship with Docker, and how their combination might usher in a new age of container orchestration.

Kubernetes, often stylized as K8s, originated from Google's decade-long experience of managing production workloads at scale. It was conceived out of the need to handle the complexities of managing containerized applications across a cluster of machines. Essentially, Kubernetes is an open-source container orchestration platform that automates containerized applications' deployment, scaling, and management. In microservices and cloud-native applications, Kubernetes emerges as the maestro, conducting a symphony of containers to ensure harmony, resilience, and high availability.

Now, where does Docker fit into this picture? Docker is primarily a platform that allows developers to containerize applications, ensuring consistency across different development lifecycle stages. In simpler terms, Docker wraps an application and its dependencies into a standardized unit known as container. These lightweight containers, devoid of the overhead typical of traditional virtual machines, are optimal for deployment. However, while Docker is phenomenal at containerization, managing these containers becomes strenuous, especially when they number in the hundreds or thousands. This is where Kubernetes steps in.

The relationship between Docker and Kubernetes can be visualized as that of a craftsman and a conductor. Docker crafts the containers precisely, ensuring every application is encased with all its dependencies, ready to run uniformly across different environments. On the other hand, Kubernetes conducts these containers, deciding where they should run, how many replicas should exist, how they should connect to each other, and how resources are allocated. It also monitors these containers and, if one fails, replaces it to ensure the application remains available to users.

One of the pivotal components in Kubernetes is the Pod. In the Kubernetes architecture, the smallest deployable unit is not the individual container but the Pod, which can house one or more containers. These containers within a Pod share the same network IP, port space, and storage, enabling them to communicate efficiently and share data. It's worth noting that while Kubernetes is not tied to Docker exclusively, Docker remains the most popular container runtime used with Kubernetes, making them frequent collaborators in many deployments.

Kubernetes also introduces a plethora of concepts that augment its orchestration capabilities. Services in Kubernetes, for instance, allow for network traffic distribution to Pods, ensuring applications remain accessible even as individual Pods are created or destroyed. ConfigMaps and Secrets enable configuration data and sensitive information to be injected into Pods, decoupling application configuration from the container image. Deployments, StatefulSets, and DaemonSets are higher-level constructs that dictate how Pods should be rolled out, updated, and maintained across the cluster.

The advantages of this symbiotic relationship between Docker and Kubernetes are manifold. For starters, scalability is elevated to new heights. With Kubernetes, scaling an application is as simple as updating a desired replica count, allowing applications to respond to varying traffic loads dynamically. Resilience is another hallmark. Kubernetes continuously monitors the health of Pods and, if it detects a failing or unresponsive container, can automatically replace it, ensuring applications are persistently available. Additionally, Kubernetes' ability to distribute containers across a cluster of machines ensures efficient resource utilization, optimizing costs and performance.

Furthermore, Kubernetes' affinity with Docker goes beyond mere orchestration. Kubernetes benefits from the vast Docker ecosystem, especially the Docker image format and the Docker Hub, a repository of container images. Using Docker's standardized image format, Kubernetes ensures that the same containerized application can run unchanged across local development machines, on-premises data centers, and various cloud environments. This universality and consistency across environments eliminate the infamous "it works on my machine" problem, streamlining development and deployment processes.

In conclusion, the dance between Kubernetes and Docker is a testament to how two groundbreaking technologies can coalesce to forge an unparalleled solution. While Docker encapsulates the intricacies of applications, ensuring they are consistently packaged and ready for deployment, Kubernetes takes on the mantle of ensuring these applications are efficiently managed, scaled, and made resilient. Together, they stand at the forefront of the container revolution, underpinning the foundations of modern, cloud-native applications. Understanding the synergy between Docker and Kubernetes is paramount for developers and enterprises looking to harness the power of containers. It's not just about containerization or orchestration in isolation; it's about crafting a seamless, efficient, and resilient application lifecycle in an ever-connected digital world.

Managed container services

The landscape of application deployment has undergone seismic shifts over the past decade. With the advent of containers, developers discovered a method to ensure application consistency across varied environments. However, while containerization resolved many challenges, it introduced a new set of complexities. Orchestrating potentially thousands of containers, ensuring their health, scalability, and security became a substantial endeavor. Cloud service providers recognized these challenges with a solution: Managed Container Services. These services are rapidly transforming how businesses approach container orchestration, offering an amalgamation of convenience, scalability, and efficiency.

At its core, Managed Container Services provide an abstraction over container orchestration platforms, offering businesses the tools they need without requiring them to manage the underlying infrastructure. Instead of grappling with the intricacies of setting up, configuring, and maintaining a container orchestration system, developers are able to concentrate on what they do best: writing code and deploying applications. These services take away the pain of infrastructure management and provide intuitive, powerful, and seamlessly integrated tools with other cloud services.

One of the driving forces behind the growing popularity of managed container solutions is their ability to reduce operational overhead drastically. Setting up a container orchestration platform, be it Kubernetes, Docker Swarm, or any other, is no trivial task. It involves many considerations – network configuration, storage solutions, and security settings. Mistakes in any of these areas can have grave implications regarding application performance and security. With Managed Container Services, much of this complexity is complicated. Cloud providers are responsible for making sure that the orchestration platform is correctly set up, updated, and secure.

The realm of security, in particular, benefits immensely from managed services. Containers, by their lightweight and transient nature, present unique security challenges. Ensuring that container images are free from vulnerabilities, that runtime environments are isolated, and that access controls are correctly implemented requires diligence. Managed Container Services often come equipped with integrated security solutions, ranging from automated vulnerability scanning and secret management to runtime security monitoring. By relying on cloud providers' expertise and vast resources, businesses can ensure that their containerized applications are efficient and secure.

Beyond security, scalability is a pivotal advantage that Managed Container Services confer. Containers are inherently scalable, but managing this scalability is another matter. Responding to varying application loads, ensuring high availability, and optimizing resource utilization require fine-tuning orchestration platforms. With their deep integrations into the cloud ecosystem, managed services can automatically scale applications based on real-time metrics. Whether it's auto-scaling the number of container instances, provisioning more storage, or adjusting network settings, these services ensure that applications can handle peak loads and quieter periods equally efficiently.

Furthermore, Managed Container Services are often deeply integrated with other cloud offerings. This integration extends the capabilities of containerized applications, allowing them to seamlessly interface with databases, analytics platforms, machine learning services, and more. For developers, this means they can craft applications that are not just containerized but also cloud-native, leveraging the full spectrum of services that cloud providers offer.

Of course, cost efficiency is one of the most substantial benefits of opting for a managed solution. Businesses can optimize their operational costs by offloading infrastructure management responsibilities to cloud providers. They no longer need to invest in hardware upfront or maintain a large team to manage the orchestration platform. Instead, they can adopt a pay-as-you-go model, paying for only the resources they use. This shift from capital expenditure to operational expenditure can lead to significant savings, particularly for businesses that experience fluctuating application loads.

Notably, most leading cloud providers, including AWS, Google Cloud, and Azure, have recognized the potential of managed container solutions and have introduced their offerings. Services like Amazon's EKS (Elastic Kubernetes Service), Google's GKE (Google Kubernetes Engine), and Azure's AKS (Azure Kubernetes Service) have become mainstays for businesses looking to deploy containerized applications at scale. While built on the foundational principles of Kubernetes, these services offer additional tools, integrations, and optimizations, making them uniquely suited for cloud-native application deployment.

In conclusion, as containerization continues to gain traction, the challenges associated with orchestrating containers at scale become increasingly evident. Managed Container Services have emerged as the de facto solution, offering businesses a pathway to deploy, scale, and manage containerized applications with unparalleled ease. By leveraging these services, businesses can free themselves from the intricacies of infrastructure management, focusing instead on innovation, growth, and delivering value to their users. As the cloud ecosystem continues to evolve, it's evident that managed solutions, especially in container orchestration, will be pivotal in shaping the future of application deployment.

CHAPTER XIII

Real-world Case Studies

Successful Docker implementations

In the ever-evolving realm of software development, the advent of Docker has signaled a transformative shift in how applications are built, deployed, as well as maintained. The rise of containerization, underpinned by Docker, has enabled organizations to overcome numerous challenges associated with traditional deployment methodologies. By embracing Docker, companies have improved their deployment pipelines' consistency, scalability, and efficiency. This section delves into various successful Docker implementations, offering a glimpse into how businesses across different sectors harness containerization's power to drive growth and innovation.

A crucial aspect of Docker's success story lies in its capacity to resolve the infamous "it works on my machine" problem. In the past, developers often encountered discrepancies between their local development environments and production settings. Such inconsistencies led to extensive debugging sessions, delayed deployments, and sometimes even critical failures in production. By introducing a uniform environment through containerization, Docker has successfully eliminated this problem. One prominent example is

Spotify, the music streaming giant. They migrated to Docker to ensure consistent environments across development and production, thereby streamlining their deployment pipeline and reducing deployment-related issues.

Beyond ensuring consistency, Docker's impact is profoundly felt in microservices. Traditional monolithic architectures posed various challenges, from slow deployment cycles to difficulties in introducing new features without affecting the entire system. The shift towards microservices, facilitated by Docker, allows businesses to develop, deploy, and scale individual components of an application independently. This architectural shift is evident in companies like Uber and Netflix, which have seamlessly transitioned to microservices using Docker. These companies have achieved accelerated development cycles, enhanced scalability, and improved fault isolation by classifying their services.

Another arena where Docker has made significant strides is in Continuous Integration and Continuous Deployment pipelines. The transient nature of Docker containers makes them ideally suited for CI/CD processes. Every code commit can spawn a fresh container, where tests are executed in a clean, controlled environment. Once tests pass, the same container can be promoted through various stages, ensuring that the tested artifact is ultimately deployed. The BBC News team employed Docker to revamp their CI/CD pipeline. By doing so, they achieved faster feedback loops, ensured consistent deployments, and drastically reduced the time to market for new features.

In the realm of big data and analytics, Docker has also found its footing. Processing vast amounts of data necessitates scalable and flexible infrastructure. Traditional virtual machines, with their overheads, often prove to be inefficient and slow. Companies like Yelp have leveraged Docker to run their big data workloads. By containerizing their data processing tasks, they've achieved faster execution times, better resource utilization, and an overall more efficient data processing pipeline.

The educational sector too hasn't remained untouched by Docker's influence. Institutions and online platforms offering coding bootcamps and courses have turned to Docker to provide their students with consistent, reproducible environments. Instead of grappling with setup instructions across varied operating systems, students can pull a Docker image and have a fully configured environment up and running in minutes. This approach streamlines the learning process and ensures that students spend their time learning critical concepts rather than troubleshooting environment-related issues.

Docker's flexibility has also benefited the scientific community, particularly in bioinformatics. Research often requires specific software versions and dependencies, leading to what's known as "dependency hell." Docker alleviates this by allowing researchers to containerize their experiments with all required dependencies. These containers can then be shared with peers, ensuring that experiments are reproducible and consistent across different research environments.

While Docker's merits are undeniable, its successful implementation isn't merely about adopting the technology; it's also about fostering a cultural shift. Companies like Capital One have recognized this. Their journey with Docker wasn't just technological; it involved retraining their workforce, embracing DevOps principles, and rethinking their application architecture from the ground up. The results, however, were worth the effort. Today, Capital One boasts a flexible, scalable, and efficient deployment infrastructure powered by Docker.

Lastly, it's essential to note that while Docker offers numerous advantages, its successful implementation requires careful planning and consideration. It's not a silver bullet, but it can bring about transformative changes when wielded correctly. Organizations need to assess their specific needs, understand Docker's nuances, and perhaps most importantly, be willing to iterate and evolve their implementation strategy as they learn.

In conclusion, Docker has undeniably revolutionized the software deployment landscape. Its impact resonates across industries, from streaming services and finance to education and scientific research. As illustrated by many examples, successful Docker implementations showcase its potential to drive efficiency, ensure consistency, and facilitate scalability. As the technology matures and evolves, it's poised to cement further its position as an indispensable tool in the modern software deployment toolkit.

Lessons learned from various projects

In the contemporary software development and deployment landscape, Docker has emerged as an indispensable tool, reshaping how organizations approach containerization. While its popularity is unquestionable, Docker's adoption across various projects has presented diverse challenges, sparking invaluable lessons for newcomers and seasoned practitioners. As businesses navigate the intricacies of Docker implementations, the collective experiences crystallize into guiding principles. This section seeks to distill the key lessons learned from various Docker projects, offering insights that can inform future endeavors.

A primary lesson that echoes across numerous Docker projects is the significance of understanding Docker's underlying principles before diving into implementation. While it might be tempting to rush into containerizing applications, appreciating Docker's architecture, the difference between an image and a container, and the nuances of Dockerfiles can prevent a host of issues down the line. Companies that jumped onto the Docker bandwagon without adequate understanding often grappled with inefficient containers, bloated images, or security vulnerabilities. The takeaway? A solid foundation in Docker's fundamentals is non-negotiable.

Another revelation from several Docker projects is the importance of optimizing Docker images. Initially, there might be a tendency to create large, all-encompassing images. However, over time, it becomes evident that such practices lead to extended build times, increased storage costs, and slower deployment cycles. Successful projects have underscored the need for minimal base images, multi-stage builds, and regular unused images and containers pruning. These optimizations streamline the deployment pipeline and bolster security by reducing the attack surface.

Speaking of security, the journey with Docker has illuminated the criticality of securing containers. Contrary to some initial beliefs, containers aren't inherently secure. As Docker projects proliferated, tales of exposed Docker daemons, unpatched images, and containers running with escalated privileges served as cautionary tales. The lessons were clear: Always follow best practices like scanning images for vulnerabilities, restricting container privileges, and using user namespaces. Moreover, tools like Docker Bench for Security and Clair have become invaluable assets for those prioritizing container security.

Networking is another realm where Docker projects have offered rich learnings. The default bridge network might suffice for rudimentary projects, but as applications grow in complexity, so do their networking needs. Successful Docker projects often revolve around custom networks, ensuring containers can communicate efficiently and securely. Additionally, understanding nuances like published ports, inter-container communication, and network drivers became essential for projects scaling across multiple hosts or needing intricate networking setups.

The allure of Docker often lies in its promise of portability — "Build once, run anywhere." However, real-world Docker projects highlight that this mantra, while generally accurate, has its caveats. Environmental differences can introduce unforeseen challenges, especially when transitioning from development to production. One poignant lesson is the value of environment-specific configurations, often managed through environment variables or configuration management tools, ensuring that Docker containers adapt seamlessly across varied environments.

Docker Compose, Docker's tool for defining and running multi-container applications, has its own set of lessons. Many projects commenced with rudimentary Docker Compose files, only to realize that as applications grew, so did the complexity of their docker-compose.yml files. Effective Docker projects often involve modular and well-organized Docker Compose configurations, leveraging features like extension fields and overrides to manage complexity and ensure maintainability.

In the storage realm, Docker volumes have presented their own challenges and insights. Initial perceptions might view them as mere storage mechanisms, but seasoned Docker projects have highlighted their multifaceted nature. Understanding the distinction between bind mounts, tmpfs mounts, and named volumes became crucial. Moreover, data persistence, backup, and restoration strategies became focal points for projects where data integrity and availability were paramount.

A more overarching lesson from Docker projects revolves around the significance of monitoring and logging. As containers are ephemeral by nature, traditional monitoring and logging approaches might fall short. Successful Docker implementations have underscored the importance of tools like Prometheus for monitoring and the ELK stack or Loki for logging. These tools, tailored for containerized environments, provide the visibility and insights essential for maintaining the health and performance of Docker deployments.

Lastly, one of the more subtle yet profound lessons from Docker's projects is the necessity of cultural adaptation. Introducing Docker isn't merely a technological shift; it necessitates changes in development practices, collaboration methodologies, and even team structures. Organizations that viewed Docker adoption solely as a tech upgrade faced friction and roadblocks. In contrast, those who embraced the cultural shifts, promoting cross-functional collaboration and continuous learning, often reaped the most benefits.

In conclusion, the journey with Docker across diverse projects has been one of continuous learning, punctuated by challenges, insights, and revelations. From understanding Docker's core principles to appreciating the intricacies of networking, storage, and security, each project has contributed to the collective wisdom surrounding Docker. As the containerization landscape continues to evolve, these lessons serve as guiding beacons, ensuring that future Docker endeavors are informed, efficient, and effective.

Conclusion

Recap of key takeaways

Reflecting upon our comprehensive journey through " Navigating Docker: From Setup to Deployment - A Developer's Companion," it's evident that Docker, and containerization at large, represent transformative technologies reshaping the fabric of software development and deployment. As we distill the wealth of knowledge acquired, let's encapsulate the crucial takeaways that stand out as guideposts for any developer venturing into the world of Docker.

To begin, understanding the foundation upon which Docker rests is imperative. Our exploration delved deep into Docker's architecture, elucidating the core components and their interplay. The distinction between Docker's images and containers, and the lifecycle and management of each, emerged as cornerstone knowledge. These constructs underpin the practical application of Docker, so their comprehension paves the way for effective containerization strategies.

Our journey through the e-book accentuated the importance of setting up Docker correctly, emphasizing the nuances of installation across different platforms, be it Windows, Mac, or Linux. It became evident that while Docker abstracts many complexities, being aware of platform-specific quirks and configurations can save considerable time and prevent potential hiccups.

The significance of Docker Hub was another salient takeaway. Serving as the central repository for Docker images, its role in facilitating collaboration, ensuring version control, and enabling the seamless distribution of containerized applications is unparalleled. Grasping the operations related to Docker Hub, especially pushing and pulling images, is indispensable for effective Docker workflows.

As we delved into practical implementations, the essence of Docker commands became evident. Basic commands, including run, build, push, and pull, form the bedrock of Docker operations. Proficiency in these commands, and understanding their nuances, empowers developers to craft, deploy, and manage containers with precision.

Managing containers emerged as a theme of its own, drawing attention to the transient nature of containers and the need for effective monitoring, logging, and orchestration strategies. Coupled with insights on networking and inter-container communication, the e-book illuminated the multifaceted nature of container operations, emphasizing that while containers offer numerous advantages, they also introduce complexities that warrant thoughtful management.

The discussion on Docker Compose highlighted the power of orchestrating multi-container applications. Writing a robust docker-compose.yml file and understanding its intricacies became a focal point, especially for projects that scale beyond single-container setups. Docker Compose's ability to streamline development environments and ensure consistent deployments stood out as a game-changer for many developers.

Dockerfile structure and best practices were central themes, highlighting the importance of crafting efficient, secure, and portable container images. The exploration into multi-stage builds, minimal base images, and strategies to reduce image sizes underscored the need for optimization, ensuring faster deployment cycles and enhanced security.

Storage strategies, mainly revolving around Docker volumes, crystallized as paramount subjects. The e-book emphasized the distinction between different storage mechanisms, alongside strategies for data persistence, backup, and restoration, equipping developers with the knowledge to handle data in containerized environments adeptly.

Security emerged as a non-negotiable theme. From running containers securely to scanning images for vulnerabilities, the e-book was replete with strategies to fortify containerized applications. Regular updates, understanding privilege escalation, and being vigilant about potential threats became the touchstones of Docker security.

Integration of Docker with CI/CD pipelines, automated testing, and deployment strategies illuminated the broader ecosystem in which Docker operates. The e-book showcased Docker's adaptability, highlighting its synergy with various tools and platforms, from Jenkins and Travis CI to cloud providers like AWS, GCP, and Azure.

A foray into Kubernetes cemented the understanding that while Docker offers incredible containerization capabilities, orchestration at scale demands robust solutions. With its powerful orchestration features, Kubernetes emerged as a natural partner to Docker, underscoring the dynamic between container creation and management.

Reflecting upon real-world scenarios, the e-book's exploration into successful Docker implementations and lessons learned from various projects provided pragmatic insights. These case studies served as cautionary tales and success stories, reminding readers of potential pitfalls and guiding them toward best practices.

In conclusion, " Navigating Docker: From Setup to Deployment - A Developer's Companion" has been a holistic voyage into the world of Docker. From foundational concepts to intricate implementation strategies, the e-book has armed readers with the knowledge and insights required to harness Docker's potential fully. As we look towards an increasingly containerized future, the lessons, strategies, and best practices elucidated in this e-book will undoubtedly serve as invaluable compasses, guiding developers toward mastery of Docker and containerization.

The growing importance of containerization

The digital age has ushered in a renaissance of software development and deployment methods. Among these, containerization is a transformative technology, quickly becoming the preferred choice for companies and developers looking to enhance their deployment strategies and development workflows. Its popularity over the last decade is more than a fleeting trend; it marks a pivotal shift in how software applications are developed, deployed, and scaled. The growing importance of containerization can be attributed to several factors, each intertwined in the broader narrative of modern software engineering.

At the heart of containerization's allure is its promise of consistency. Traditional software deployment often carried the risk of the dreaded "it works on my machine" problem. This challenge arose due to differences in development, staging, and production environments, leading to unforeseen bugs and incompatibilities. Containers ushered in a solution to this age-old problem by packaging an application and its dependencies into a singular unit, ensuring the application behaves consistently across various environments. This uniformity simplifies the development lifecycle, dramatically reducing the likelihood of environment-specific anomalies.

Furthermore, the flexibility and scalability afforded by containerization are unparalleled. In the pre-container era, scaling applications typically duplicated the entire server environment, leading to resource wastage and increased costs. Containers, being lightweight, allow for efficient use of system resources. An application, when containerized, can be replicated easily across multiple instances, facilitating horizontal scaling. This granular control over application instances is especially beneficial for microservices architectures, where different services can be containerized and scaled independently based on demand.

Beyond scalability, containerization offers rapid deployment and rollback capabilities. Since containers encapsulate all necessary binaries and libraries, spinning up a new instance or rolling back to a previous version becomes almost instantaneous. This speed is crucial in today's agile and DevOps-driven world, where continuous integration and continuous delivery (CI/CD) pipelines necessitate quick and reliable deployments. Integrating containerization into CI/CD pipelines streamlines the software delivery process, fostering a culture of rapid iteration and feedback.

The isolation provided by containers also contributes to their growing importance. Each container runs in an isolated environment, ensuring that the operations of one do not interfere with others. This segregation is vital for security, as potential breaches or vulnerabilities in one container do not compromise the entire system. Moreover, isolation ensures that applications have dedicated resources, guaranteeing performance consistency.

Economic considerations further bolster containerization's significance. Traditional virtualization methods, like using virtual machines (VMs), often led to underutilized resources. Containers, in contrast, share the host system's OS kernel, negating the need for multiple OS instances. This efficiency translates to cost savings, especially in cloud environments where compute resources are billed based on usage.

Tools like Docker and Kubernetes have become synonymous with modern software deployment strategies in the containerization ecosystem. Docker simplifies creating, deploying, and running applications in containers. Its user-friendly nature, combined with a rich set of features, has made it the de facto standard for containerization. On the other hand, Kubernetes, a container orchestration platform, handles containerized applications' deployment, scaling, and management, addressing the complexities that arise when applications scale.

The community and ecosystem that have grown around containerization tools are also noteworthy. The containerization landscape is rich with resources that facilitate learning and implementation, from plugins, extensions, and integrations with other software tools to comprehensive documentation and vibrant community support.

Furthermore, the adaptability of containerization to diverse use cases enhances its importance. From startups to tech giants, organizations of all sizes and across industries are leveraging containerization for various applications, be it web services, data analytics, or machine learning workloads. This universality testifies to the technology's robustness and relevance in an ever-evolving software landscape.

Finally, looking to the future, the trajectory of containerization appears even more promising. As edge computing gains traction, containers are poised to play a pivotal role, given their lightweight nature, making them suitable for resource-constrained edge devices. Similarly, as multicloud strategies become more prevalent, containerization provides a consistent deployment method across different cloud providers, ensuring portability and reducing vendor lock-in.

In conclusion, the importance of containerization in today's software landscape cannot be overstated. As a paradigm, it encapsulates the essence of modern software development and deployment practices – consistency, scalability, flexibility, and efficiency. As organizations continue to recognize the manifold benefits of containerization, it's evident that this technology will remain at the forefront of software innovation, guiding the industry toward more streamlined, efficient, and effective solutions.

The future roadmap for Docker

Since its inception, Docker has revolutionized the software development landscape with its innovative approach to containerization. It has grown from a niche tool to a full-fledged ecosystem, helping businesses and developers embrace containerized applications' agility, consistency, and scalability. As with any dynamic technology, speculating about Docker's future involves examining the current trends, challenges, and evolving needs of the developer community and broader industry. Based on these dimensions, this section delves into the potential future roadmap for Docker.

From the outset, it's essential to recognize that Docker's success has always been intertwined with the broader container ecosystem. Kubernetes, for instance, has become the gold standard for container orchestration. While Docker Swarm, Docker's native clustering and orchestration tool, offers many functionalities, Kubernetes stands out for its extensibility and vast community support. Recognizing this, Docker has already started focusing on improving integration with

Kubernetes, ensuring that developers can seamlessly deploy Docker containers within Kubernetes clusters. We can anticipate that Docker's future roadmap will involve even tighter integration with Kubernetes, offering tools and features that streamline the deployment and management process for developers.

Security remains paramount in the software development realm, and Docker is no exception. The nature of containers — sharing the host's operating system kernel — presents unique security challenges. While Docker has made significant strides in enhancing container security, there is always room for improvement. Future iterations of Docker might offer improved security features, such as more robust isolation mechanisms, better vulnerability scanning tools, and integrations with leading enterprise security solutions. Additionally, with the rise of confidential computing and hardware-level security, Docker might delve deeper into leveraging hardware-based solutions to ensure container integrity and confidentiality.

Performance optimization will likely be another focal area. While containers are inherently lightweight, there are opportunities to make them even more efficient, particularly in microservices architectures where thousands of containers might be running concurrently. Future Docker updates might offer improved resource allocation algorithms, tools to identify and rectify performance bottlenecks, and integrations with platforms that optimize real-time container performance.

Docker's extensibility and plugin architecture have been among its key strengths. The rich ecosystem of plugins, ranging from networking to storage to monitoring, has allowed developers to tailor the Docker experience to their specific needs. As the developer community's needs evolve and diversify, Docker's roadmap will likely focus on making the platform even more extensible. We might see a more vibrant marketplace for Docker plugins, with Docker Inc. fostering a community where third-party developers can contribute and monetize their solutions.

Edge computing is an appearing paradigm that pushes computation closer to the data source, whether IoT or other edge devices. Given the resource constraints typical of edge devices, lightweight computational solutions are essential. Docker's containerization approach is ideally suited for this. The future might see Docker releasing features and optimizations tailored for edge environments, ensuring containers can run efficiently even on low-power devices.

Another noteworthy trend is the rise of serverless computing. While it might seem at odds with containerization, there's a convergence happening. Developers want the agility of serverless — deploying code without managing the underlying infrastructure — while still leveraging the consistency and control that containers offer. Docker could potentially venture into this space, offering solutions that bring the best of both worlds — the flexibility of serverless and the predictability of containers.

One challenge Docker has faced is the size of container images. Although containers are more lightweight than virtual machines, the images can still be hefty, especially when not optimized. As a response to this, Docker might double down on efforts to optimize image sizes further, possibly introducing features that automatically trim down unnecessary components or suggest optimizations to developers.

Multi-cloud strategies are becoming increasingly common among enterprises, driven by a desire to avoid vendor lock-in and leverage the best features of different cloud providers. Given its portability benefits, Docker plays a pivotal role in such strategies. In the future, Docker might offer enhanced tools that simplify multi-cloud deployments, ensuring that Docker containers run seamlessly across diverse cloud environments.

Finally, it's essential to consider the business aspect. Docker Inc., the company behind Docker, has undergone significant changes, including a refocus on the developer community and enterprise solutions. Its future roadmap will be influenced by its business strategy. This might involve offering more enterprise-centric features, premium support options, and solutions catering to large organizations' needs.

In conclusion, Docker's journey has been nothing short of transformative for the software industry. As we gaze into the future, it's clear that Docker's potential remains vast. Whether it's tighter integrations with other platforms, security enhancements, or optimizations for emerging computing paradigms, Docker is poised to stay at the forefront of containerization solutions. Its roadmap will undoubtedly be shaped by both the evolving needs of the developer community and the broader shifts in the software and business landscapes. Whatever the direction, Docker's commitment to innovation, community, and excellence is likely to remain unwavering.

Final thoughts for developers

In today's rapidly evolving technological landscape, developers stand at the forefront of shaping the digital future. Their decisions, expertise, and ability to adapt determine the trajectory of their careers and the direction in which industries move. As we conclude our extensive exploration of Docker and delve into broader implications for developers, several fundamental takeaways and reflections are worth considering.

To begin with, it's evident that the role of a developer has transcended mere coding. Modern developers are now expected to be interdisciplinary experts, capable of understanding infrastructure, networking, security, and even business logic. The rise of tools like Docker underscores this transition. Developers are no longer just infrastructure users; they play a pivotal role in defining it. This expanded responsibility brings opportunities and challenges in equal measure. Opportunities lie in the newfound power to shape entire application landscapes, while challenges arise from the breadth of knowledge now required. For budding and veteran developers alike, continuous learning is no longer optional but imperative.

The embrace of containerization and the broader microservices paradigm brings about another key reflection: the shift from monolithic structures to modular components. This architectural transition mirrors broader changes in how software and solutions are conceived. Modularity, scalability, and flexibility are now prime objectives. Developers must, therefore, train themselves to think in terms of systems, not just standalone applications. This system-level thinking ensures that individual components, though developed independently, can interact harmoniously within a larger framework. Furthermore, the focus on modularity also means that developers must pay greater attention to interfaces, contracts, and communication between different software elements.

Another significant takeaway is the emphasis on collaboration. Tools like Docker, while technical in nature, are also inherently collaborative. They facilitate smoother interactions between development, operations, and other teams. In a way, the rise of such tools highlights the dissolution of rigid silos. Developers can no longer afford to work in isolation. Collaboration is not just about working with other developers but extends to cross-functional teams. Engaging with operations, security, business, and even end-users becomes essential. The open-source ethos that pervades tools like Docker further emphasizes this collaborative spirit. Participating actively in the community, sharing insights, and learning from peers worldwide can enrich a developer's journey immensely.

Security, often a secondary concern in earlier development paradigms, now takes center stage. With breaches, vulnerabilities, and cyber threats becoming increasingly sophisticated, developers have a pivotal role in building and maintaining secure applications. Tools and practices evolve, but a security-first mindset becomes crucial, where security is an integral part of the development lifecycle and not an afterthought. This mindset extends from writing secure code to understanding and implementing best practices in containerization, deployment, and continuous integration.

Yet, even as we advocate for adopting new tools and paradigms, striking a balance is essential. Brimming with innovations, the tech industry sometimes leads developers into a trap of perennially chasing the "next big thing." While staying updated is crucial, it's equally vital to master the fundamentals. Understanding the underlying principles of software development, databases, networking, and system design can provide a strong foundation for exploring and adapting to new technologies. Mastery of the basics ensures that developers can judiciously choose the right tool for the right job, rather than being swayed by every fleeting trend.

The importance of soft skills is another aspect that warrants attention. While technical prowess is undeniably vital, communicating effectively, empathizing with users and team members, and understanding business objectives can set a developer apart. As solutions become more user-centric, a developer's ability to understand and cater to user needs, pain points, and aspirations becomes invaluable. Additionally, as remote work and distributed teams become more prevalent, effective communication and collaboration skills become indispensable.

Finally, it's worth reflecting on the broader implications of a developer's work. Every line of code, application, and system profoundly impacts individuals, societies, and economies in an increasingly digital world. Ethical considerations, therefore, must be integral to a developer's thought process. From ensuring user privacy and data security to understanding the socio-economic implications of algorithms and applications, developers wield significant power and bear immense responsibility.

In conclusion, several guiding principles emerge as developers navigate the multifaceted landscape of modern software development. Among the critical pillars are embracing continuous learning, fostering collaboration, prioritizing security, mastering the basics, honing soft skills, and adhering to ethical standards. Tools, technologies, and paradigms will evolve, but these foundational principles will remain steadfast. As we stand at the cusp of exciting technological advancements, with innovations like Docker leading the charge, developers have both an opportunity and a responsibility. The opportunity lies in shaping the digital future, and the responsibility rests in ensuring that this future is inclusive, secure, and beneficial for all.

Thank you for buying and reading/listening to our book. If you found this book useful/helpful please take a few minutes and leave a review on the platform where you purchased our book. Your feedback matters greatly to us.